Proofr[...]

Plain and Simple

By
Debra Hart May

CAREER PRESS
3 Tice Road
P.O. Box 687
Franklin Lakes, NJ 07417
1-800-CAREER-1
201-848-0310 (NJ and outside U.S.)
FAX: 201-848-1727

PROOFREADING PLAIN AND SIMPLE

Cover design by The Hub Graphics Corp.
Printed in the U.S.A. by Book-mart Press

To order this title by mail, please include price as noted above, $2.50 handling per order, and $1.50 for each book ordered. Send to: Career Press, Inc., 3 Tice Road, P.O. Box 687, Franklin Lakes, NJ 07417.

Or call toll-free 1-800-CAREER-1 (NJ and Canada: 201-848-0310) to order using VISA or MasterCard, or for further information on books from Career Press.

Library of Congress Cataloging-in-Publication Data
May, Debra Hart, 1961-
    Proofreading plain and simple / by Debra Hart May.
        p.   cm.
    Includes index.
    ISBN 1-56414-291-4 (pbk.)
    1. Proofreading--United States. 2. Business writing--United States. 3. English language--United States--Business English.
    I. Title.
Z254.M48 1997
686.2'255--dc21   97-8273
                                                              CIP

To my parents, for their quiet, but constant support.

Acknowledgments

This book is the product of the insights and contributions of many people. I'd like to thank the following people who, knowingly or not, had much to do with its realization.

I'm deeply grateful to those (I could list by the dozens, so forgive me if I do not) who provided insights into their own editing, proofreading, and writing processes. Special thanks to my colleagues, especially Linda Comerford and Dr. Harriet Wilkins, for their endless resourcefulness, encouragement, and mentoring.

Thanks to my students and clients, who supplied me with stories and examples and who continue to challenge and teach me.

Thanks, too, to my patient but harried editors and—of course—this book's proofreaders.

To my friends, thanks for your unquestioning confidence in me and your patience as this book became the center of my universe for a short while.

Finally, to my husband, thank you for your tolerance, your loving support, and your quirky indulgence in my interests as a "Writing Nerd."

Contents

Introduction

Do you proofread? Do you really and consistently proofread? If you've ever been called on a transposed number, a wrong date, or perhaps you even caught yourself leaving some significant detail out of a memo, a letter, or even a personal party invitation, chances are you didn't really proofread it. Oh, you probably looked it over. Only the foolhardy fail to take a second look. But proofreading any written document requires more than just glancing it over before sending it out (or worse, mass producing it). If getting it right is truly important, proofreading is the strategy to get it there.

But most of us never learned to proofread. And proofreading, let's face it, isn't much fun. It's tedious and requires uninterrupted concentration.

Benefits of proofreading well

Proofreading well, however, may well be worth it to you. Proofreading well can save you the time it takes to explain yourself to those who got your memo or e-mail message and weren't quite sure what you meant. It can save you and others the headaches and embarrassment caused by information in a letter that someone understood one way but you intended another. It can even save you money. (Transposed numbers following dollar signs can be especially dangerous. So can advertising copy that makes promises you didn't intend to make.) Proofreading well can even save a life. (Imagine a 911 operator sending a rescue vehicle to 5324 Maple when the heart attack was occurring at 5342 Maple.)

How this book can help

This book can help you proofread more effectively. It can help you catch and correct every potentially embarrassing, troublesome, or costly error. Because proofreading is a challenge for most of us, and because so few of us really know how to do it, this book offers you help with knowing:

- ◆ What to look for.
- ◆ When to look for it.
- ◆ How to look for it.
- ◆ How to handle what you find.

This is not a grammar book. It's also not a book on punctuation, spelling, or capitalization. But it does address those issues and provide plenty of suggestions for improving your skills with these and other aspects of the English language. Furthermore, as we explore the *most critical* and *most common* errors people tend to make when they write, we will take short detours into all of these areas.

We'll also explore other issues that can make proofreading especially challenging: How do you find the time to do it? How do you tactfully handle proofreading for someone else (especially if it's your boss)? How important is proofreading when it comes to e-mail and other forms of online communication? Can you proofread proficiently if you're a poor speller? What if those comma rules continue to elude you? By reading *Proofreading Plain and Simple* you will be able to resolve these issues with confidence.

How to use this book

Read this book to build your overall understanding and mastery of proofreading skills. Read it cover to cover, or focus on the chapters that are most useful to you. Here is what you will find in each chapter:

Chapter One further explores what proofreading is and why it's important.

Chapter Two covers the aptitudes, skills, knowledge, and strategies the experts consider necessary for effective proofreading. In this chapter I will introduce an "expert's approach" to proofreading: the steps professional proofreaders suggest as the most effective.

Chapter Three discusses the mental gymnastics we must undergo to proofread effectively and basic steps you can take to prepare both your mind and your environment so you can proofread most effectively.

Chapter Four provides a detailed approach to editing any important document; editing is the step that should precede proofreading. Look for a review of key grammar points in this chapter.

Chapter Five takes you through a series of skill development exercises to help you use the tools professional proofreaders and editors use: proofreaders' marks. By chapter's end you'll have acquired a new set of tools for communicating when proofreading.

Chapter Six helps you decide where to focus your time and energy during each step of the professionals' proofreading process. You'll learn what to look for, when, and how.

Chapter Seven provides some quick help on the punctuation errors most people find troublesome; as a proofreader, you may find these errors either most prevalent or most difficult to catch (especially if you're unclear on the rules yourself).

Chapter Eight explores the unique challenges inherent in proofreading on screen, whether you're proofreading an electronic file, e-mail message, or online communication.

Chapter Nine suggests *do's* and *don'ts* when you're proofreading for other people. A critical part of proofreading for others involves maneuvering the interpersonal challenges it may create for you.

Improving any skill takes time and practice. *Proofreading Plain and Simple* will give you a solid starting point towards not just improving the skills needed for proofreading, but for mastering them as well.

By learning the time-tested methods presented here, you will be able to ensure complete accuracy in any written communication, especially when it absolutely, positively has to be flawless.

1

Can better proofreading skills help you?

We've all been there: You finally get that important letter, fax, or e-mail message off, and you think, "Mission accomplished." Then you find some reason to look back at what you wrote, and—oops!—you realize you left out an important word. Or (more embarrassing) you've left an extra word in—the ghost of a first phrasing. Or (the absolute worst!) you misspelled the recipient's company name!

Perhaps you pride yourself on being accurate. And because a small error in any document, on paper or on screen, can make a whoppingly bad impression, you proofread absolutely everything that leaves your hand or computer screen, right? And nothing, but nothing, escapes your critical eye.

If so, congratulations. But most of us neglect the important last stage of any business writing project—we fail to proofread. Or we fail to proofread well. It may be because we're in a hurry, or because after putting a lot of thought into the message itself and feeling good about it, we just don't bother taking one more good look. For many of us, it may be that we've never been clear about how to proofread effectively and we aren't confident checking our own grammar and punctuation (an estimated 80 percent of business professionals aren't!).

Whatever the reason, failing to proofread effectively means at least a little embarrassment for the writer. For the writer's company, it can mean bad public relations and even financial liabilities. Consider how it would affect a job hunter's prospects if his or her resume was not thoroughly proofread and contained, among other errors, a misspelling of the company's name to which it was sent. Errors resulting from a failure to proofread almost always mean a mangled or missed communication, and even a missed opportunity.

Consider the embarrassment this newspaper headline writer must have felt upon realizing what this headline really said:

"Tuna Biting Off the Coast
of Washington"

Or how about the notoriety, and perhaps the touch of bad public relations, that can be the result of ineffective proofreading. Consider the dilemma the Olfa Corporation faced when this warning appeared on a knife blade it manufactured:

"Caution: Blade is
extremely sharp! Keep out
of children!"

Finally, consider the situation our government got itself into when an unidentified congressional clerk was instructed to write:

> "All foreign fruit-plants are
> free from duty."

Instead he wrote:

> "All foreign fruit, plants are
> free from duty."

This one mistaken mark of punctuation cost the U.S. government $2 million before a new session of Congress could rectify the error.

How about *your* writing? Is it free from costly or embarrassing errors? This book can help you if:

- ◆ You feel that your writing makes a strong impression—good or bad.

- ◆ You've embarrassed yourself at least on occasion with a typo or other obvious mistake.

- ◆ You often must produce documents quickly.

- ◆ Your writing time is typically limited.

- ◆ You can't always rely on the proofreading skills of a competent assistant or secretary.

- ◆ You are the assistant or secretary and you're always looking for new tips.

- ◆ You've become computer literate and, with or without top-notch grammar skills, you compose letters, memos, faxes, and e-mail on computer.

- ◆ You're faced with proofreading highly technical information, the language of which you may not always comprehend.

♦ You're a student hoping to one day find gainful employment and, therefore, could use a few tips on polishing up those reports and term papers.

♦ You're ready to find gainful employment and need a professional, polished resume to help you make a good impression.

If any or all of these conditions exist for you, this book can help!

Is proofreading really that important?

Our English teachers made it clear that they thought proofreading was important. Back in school certain types of errors in the final draft of a composition brought dire consequences, or so they seemed back then: even the drop of a letter grade or two! When I taught English composition at a large state university in the early 80s, my department's policy was to routinely award a D to any paper with a single comma splice or run-on (two ways we mistakenly run together the separate ideas in a compound sentence)—both the result of simple punctuation errors. (For more on comma splices and run-ons, see Chapter 4.)

But were those standards a little high? Once most people get through freshman composition and eventually move into an occupation in which they're more often judged for other skills, so what if their writing skills still aren't up to an English teacher's standards? I know plenty of successful middle managers in large corporations—and even a few executives—whose writing skills would make most English teachers cringe. So how important are good writing skills, let alone good proofreading skills, after you leave school?

A key to success in business

Good communication skills matter in business. In study after study, when executives are asked to identify those skills most critical to succeeding in business, they nearly always choose communication skills first. And several years ago, the American Society of Training and Development determined that business writing and editing skills were the second most requested training topic by business professionals in the U.S. (The most requested topic was technical skills specific to their professions.)

And our English teachers were right about something else: When executives throughout the U.S. were asked which grammar errors in writing made the worst impression, they identified the comma splice or run-on as being among the worst errors. (Both can be avoided with good proofreading skills.) Poor or careless writing communicates volumes.

Small errors, big effects

Think of the last careless writing error you caught someone else make in a written communication to you. Maybe a day and date didn't match up: a meeting was set for Wednesday, the 17th, but the 17th day of the month was really Tuesday; maybe a *your* turned out to be a *you*; maybe a name was misspelled. What effect did that simple error have on you? One of three things probably happened.

Perhaps you accepted the misinformation, or some part of it, without thinking too much about it. You showed up for your meeting on Wednesday only to find that it had happened the day before. That little error certainly affected you!

Or perhaps you caught the error, and it threw you off track. Say you stumbled over the *you* intended to be a *your:* "You support is imperative if we are to meet our goals." If your mind wandered at all, the effect of the message was lost! Communications experts call this phenomenon "semantic noise": some aspect of the language, intended to be the invisible medium for getting the message across, instead draws our attention away from the message. We pay more attention to the noise (in this case, the typo) than the message, and the message loses its impact.

The third effect that simple error may have had on you is perhaps the most detrimental to its author: It led you to make a snap judgment about the author. At the very least, you decided he or she was careless, imprecise, or too busy. If it's a glaring or important error, you may even have judged the author incompetent. Or in the case of your misspelled name, you may have decided that he or she simply doesn't care about you.

The sad truth about simple proofreading errors is that they always make an impression, and never a good one. Recently a colleague wrote me to confirm that I'd participate as a workshop panelist during a day-long conference. The letter looked sharp: From her company letterhead to her polite-but-down-to-business tone, this was one impressive business communication—until I turned the page. There on page two was an equally well-crafted send-off paragraph thanking me again for "agreeing to provide the keynote address." Boy, was I surprised! Of course, I quickly realized she'd probably whipped off a series of these letters, changing only key pieces of information in each to suit each recipient's situation.

But I had to chuckle. What version had the keynote speaker received if I'd received hers?

What is proofreading?

A common misperception in business is that if you write, you naturally proofread. Proofreading is simply looking over a document before sending it or sending it out, right? Wrong. Most of us naturally glance back over what we've written to check for accuracy. But re-reading is not proofreading.

The term *proofreader* originated in the printing industry, where one or more individuals were hired strictly to check for typographical errors on *proofs*, or the first runs of printed copy. It was, and still is, a critical job in the printing process. Mistakes not corrected at this stage can be costly. (No wonder *National Geographic* typically has four proofreaders each read an article four times!)

Today, whether you work in the printing industry or elsewhere, true proofreading means ensuring that no errors in communication make it to the reader. And proofreading takes a set of skills that can be learned, practiced, and developed. Or neglected.

In fact, many of us who have neglected, and maybe even downplayed, the importance of good proofreading (perhaps because in the past we had an administrative assistant to do it for us) have found we're less prepared than we'd like to be to handle the job ourselves.

Corporate downsizing, flatter organizational structures, and increased access to computers as communications devices have meant most of us are often on our own with our writing projects, start to finish. If your overall writing skills need work, you've probably already gone looking for help to develop those skills. (A vast majority of business professionals have, according to the American Society of Training and Development's research.) But those of us who have long believed that proofreading just comes naturally may be shocked to learned how poor a job we're doing.

Yes, I said "we." Even competent writers have trouble with an anti-proofreading mind-set. Even if you're pretty confident with your writing skills, I'll bet you can name a time a really obvious mistake came back to bite you. Okay, I'll start. I make my living writing and editing, but in the last year I've had two—no, three—different clients tactfully inform me I'd misused their organizations' names! One organization did something quirky with capitalization in its name; the other two had undergone minor name changes within the year, and I got caught using the old versions. Whoops!

The point is that we all get busy, take shortcuts, assume we're on top of the simple things, and at times *fail to proofread*. And if we don't view proofreading as a set of skills we must decide to practice and develop, we'll simply never get much better at it and probably never truly be able to trust our professional image or how well we're communicating.

2

Proofreading advice from the experts

Because most of us are only periodic proofreaders, let's look to the experts, people who work every day as professional proofreaders in the publishing field, for some solid advice.

If true proofreading means making sure no errors get through, how do we accomplish this? According to the experts I've spoken with, having the right mind-set about proofreading is naturally just the first step. From there your success or failure lies in:

- ◆ Your aptitude for proofreading.

- ◆ Your mastery of particular skills and knowledge relevant to proofreading.

- ◆ Your specific approach.

- ◆ Your environment.

We'll address the basic tenets of the first three topics in this chapter, one at a time. Environment is fully addressed in Chapter 3.

1. The aptitude for proofreading

Anyone can improve his or her proofreading skills. But some people seem to have a natural aptitude for this very demanding work. If you've found yourself having to do a lot of writing, proofreading may be becoming more of an issue for you. And if you've suspected that other people seem naturally better suited to proofread, you may be right.

Proofreading requires intense, focused concentration. Proofreading requires extreme attention to detail. Proofreading requires persistence to keep focused on information that may not be the most interesting or entertaining. Proofreading may feel like a roadblock to getting important things done quickly. Proofreading requires that you know and use the basic tenets of the English language with confidence. And it requires sitting in the same spot for at least 20 minutes at a time.

If, as you read this list of characteristics, you thought to yourself, "Hey, no problem. I may just be cut out for proofreading," great! In fact, if your boss or co-workers haven't already started seeking you out to help them proofread their stuff, you may want to consider offering your services. Why would I suggest such a crazy idea when your time is already at a premium? For two reasons.

The first is job security. These days few professionals keep a job long or continue to get promoted without proving their versatility by demonstrating a number of invaluable talents to their bosses and co-workers. Being a skilled proofreader helps make you invaluable to those around you.

The second reason is that helping your colleagues, especially the 80 percent or so who still struggle some with the written word, can have big payoffs. The payoffs are called business relationships, and they're what you probably rely on most to help you get done what you need to get done. One-on-one help with a computer problem, a rush order from the copy room, quick marketing advice—who would have thought that offering up a little proofreading could help you become a more effective working professional? Try it. And trade proofreading favors, too. When you're the author, there's no better way to proofread than to ask someone else, someone whose skills you trust, to proofread for you. We'll discuss all the good reasons for this sound advice in the Chapter 3.

Okay, but what if you sense that you don't have the aptitude for proofreading? What if those characteristics describing the job of proofreading (several paragraphs back) turned your stomach?

Unfortunately, that rarely means you're off the hook—unless, of course, you're fortunate enough to have an assistant. If you're not one of those fortunate few, my advice is: Regardless of your inherent aptitude for proofreading, focus on learning the skills and knowledge proofreading demands.

2. The skills and knowledge for proofreading

To address skills and knowledge needed for proofreading, let's take a closer look at what the job of proofreading entails. Writing professionals often make a distinction between editing and proofreading. So let's begin by distinguishing between the two.

Editing is the writing task immediately preceding proofreading that attempts to ensure that the writer's fundamental message comes across as effectively as possible. Editing generally requires rewriting bits and pieces, and perhaps major sections, of a document typically with the following goals in mind:

♦ Clarity of thought.

♦ Attention to the reader's needs.

♦ Clear expression of the document's purpose.

♦ Accuracy of information.

♦ Appropriateness of tone.

♦ Effective use of language (word choice, etc.).

♦ Conciseness.

Those of us in relatively autonomous technical or professional positions probably handle this task ourselves. If your role is less autonomous, you may be blessed with a supervisor or manager who helps you along with his or her red pen. That's editing, for better or worse. It's a critical first step to cleaning up any document draft, so critical in fact that in the publishing industry, different individuals (and often many individuals) take on the separate roles of writing, editing, and proofreading. See Chapter 4 for advice on effective editing strategies.

Proofreading, on the other hand, involves making only minor changes, additions, or deletions to a document, but no major rewriting. Professional proofreaders categorize all or most of the following as primary goals when proofreading standard types of business communications. You would be well-served when proofreading to have developed skills and knowledge in these areas:

- Spelling.
- Punctuation.
- Capitalization.
- Typographical errors.
- Correct and consistent use of language.
- Adherence to an established style and format.
- Professional appearance.

Think of proofreading as putting a fresh coat of paint on a clean, scraped, prepared wall. It finishes up the final appearance and impression. Edit first to "prepare your wall," and then proofread to finish a document off with that "fresh coat of paint."

3. Your proofreading approach

How you go about your proofreading also plays a role in how successful you'll be.

Two basic methods

If you're the typical business professional, you'll find yourself using one of two basic methods of proofreading in different circumstances and at different stages of the proofreading process. In any typical proofreading situation, you'll first *direct* proofread, also called *noncomparison* or *dry* proofreading, which means marking changes while looking at just one document.

If you take the experts' advice and always proofread first on paper, you may then need to *comparison* proofread, which means comparing two documents, in this case one on paper and the other on screen, marking or changing one (e.g., the on-screen version) to match the other (e.g., the paper version with your changes). Here are some tips for handling both types of proofreading situations.

Direct proofreading. Most of your proofreading time will probably take the form of direct proofreading, working alone and with only one document. And here no two professional proofreaders agree on a single best approach. But their approaches do contain some common elements. The experts agree on the following points:

♦ Proofreading quickly and well is virtually impossible. To proofread most effectively, read slowly and deliberately.

♦ Catching everything requires proofreading in several stages, typically focusing on particular aspects of the writing at each stage.

♦ Proofreading your own work is difficult because you are likely to see what you meant to write as opposed to what is actually on the paper. Always allow time between editing and proofreading.

♦ Proofreading on a paper copy may be inconvenient, but you'll catch more, more quickly, and with less effort. Freelance editor and writer Helen O'Guinn summed up most experts' sentiments: "I will catch errors on paper that I will *never* catch on screen."

♦ Using the computer spell-check feature before you start can help save you a lot time.

♦ Using computerized grammar checkers are generally not helpful. Even documents considered well-written by most people, take for instance, *The Gettysburg Address*, qualify as poorly written if we're to trust the judgment of most grammar-checking software currently available.

Comparison proofreading. When comparison proof-reading, an extra tool or two can help you increase your odds of catching all the errors. Plastic document holders that attach to your computer have ruler-like guides to help you keep your place. If you do much comparison proofreading at all, these are a small investment well worth the cost.

At the very least, a ruler can help accomplish the same purpose on a flat surface. Place the documents as close together as possible and isolate individual lines of the corrected document a few at a time. A pencil, finger, or second ruler can help you keep your place on a second document if it's not on computer. When your second document is on computer, use your cursor and the parameters of your screen or document window to help you keep focus on a small segment of the document at a time. For on-screen proofreading tips, see Chapter 8.

Partner proofreading is also an option. In partner proofreading, one person reads from the corrected document, punctuation and all, and the other person makes corrections on a second document or on computer. Partner proofreading does take extra manpower, but it may well be worth the effort. Two people tend to catch errors faster, and the proofreading becomes less tedious.

Many of my writer and writing instructor colleagues and I have found both partner proofreading and partner editing, using either one or two copies of a document, extremely valuable. Reading your own work aloud for another's critique helps you both hear problems in the writing (such as a negative tone, repetitiveness, poor word choice) that may not be apparent on the printed page. In the same way, when drafting a document, expressing your ideas out loud can help you develop them into coherent thoughts.

Mac voice

My colleague and author of another book in this series, *Punctuation Plain and Simple,* Edgar C. Alward, recommends listening as someone else reads your draft to you. I've used this strategy and it can be remarkably enlightening!

The experts' approach

Here are the steps professional proofreaders typically take when direct proofreading:

1. **Read the entire document**—or a good-sized chunk of a larger document—once slowly, reading for overall content and meaning.

   At this stage check only for how understandable the document is. Even if an editor has already checked it, does it make sense to you? Would it make sense to its recipient? Does it flow easily from one idea to the next? Circle any rough spots or areas that raise questions, but don't attempt to correct every small error. If you're proofreading for someone else, stop at this point and address any questions to the editor or author. For additional important advice on proofreading for other people, see Chapter 9.

2. **Read the document again, this time *aloud*** and even more slowly, correcting all errors you find.

   You may need to isolate yourself to read aloud (a good idea anyway), but there's nothing like it to catch errors. Author Eudora Welty found this technique useful in the 70s when she toured the country reading her work aloud for the first time.

Reading aloud will especially help you catch errors of sentence structure, grammar, some punctuation, word choice, unnecessary repetitiveness, some typographical errors, and even tone. Much of these issues really should have been uncovered at the editing stage, but as proofreader, you're looking for anything missed in a previous stage. As writing consultant Lorraine Seabrook put it, "The ear helps you catch what the eye misses."

Editor Helen O'Guinn always whispers numbers out loud when she's proofreading because number errors are especially difficult to catch. She also uses a technique I see used often among professional proofreaders: She moves one finger along the text as she reads, when necessary, exposing one single character at a time.

3. **Read the document a third time,** silently, focusing especially on trouble spots.

   At this stage the proofreader's goal is to attempt to comb through the text, word by word and letter by letter, dissecting it rather than comprehending it. Chapter 6 addresses trouble spots that are especially common or critical. For now, here are some common ones:

   ♦ Transposed numbers in dates or figures.

   ♦ Errors in columns of numbers.

   ♦ Incorrect months, days, or years in dates.

   ♦ Misspelled proper names (especially of people, organizations, or product or program names).

- Typos—hard to catch because our brain typically allows us to see what we want to see (e.g., *an* for *and*, *or* for *of*, *to* for *the*, and *you* for *your*).

- Punctuation errors (e.g., overuse of commas and underuse of apostrophes and hyphens).

- Words incorrectly capitalized.

- Words often confused (e.g., *affect* versus *effect*).

- Subjects and verbs that don't agree, typically found in long sentences, even though they sound fine.

- Inconsistent verb tenses (e.g., past tense to present).

- Misnumbered sequences.

- Missing titles, labels, or legends in charts or graphs.

- Connected references (e.g., page numbers on a table of contents page, footnotes and their notations).

- Missing parts of a document (e.g., the date or return address on a letter).

- Inconsistent use of abbreviations, spacing, and format.

Proofreaders should also be careful at this stage to check for inconsistent use of proper names; appropriate use of trademarks and copyrights; inconsistent or missing references; inconsistencies in the use of headings, fonts, boldface, and italics; and other issues that don't arise too often, but are important to be aware of nevertheless.

4. **Read the document backwards.** Note, however, that the verdict's still out on the value of taking this fourth step.

Many say there's no better way to check for spelling and a few other hard-to-catch types of errors. Edgar Alward uses this technique to overcome a tendency we all have when reading forward. As he explains, "We don't read word for word. If you photograph someone reading, you'll see his or her eyes covering entire phrases and clauses at a time. In fact, the wider the eye span, the more rapidly someone reads." And unless you're looking at every letter of every word, you're unlikely to see many types of errors.

But while reading backwards can certainly help, the technique is as prone to missing certain kinds of spelling errors as any good computer spell-checker. Homonyms (for example, *to, two,* and *too*), misspelled words that happen to form other perfectly good words (for example, *form* in place of *from*), words ending in an *s* or *ly* that shouldn't, or words missing altogether: None of these will likely become evident when you're reading backwards. In addition, reading backwards is extremely tedious. One proofreading handbook for publishing professionals even calls reading backwards "unnecessary torture." Personally, I must agree; I honestly rarely do it.

5. **Scan the document at arm's length.** Some of the most blatant, poor-impression-making errors can remain invisible until you pull back and

consider the overall look and effectiveness of a page or document. What kind of impression does it make? Does it look enticing to read? (For instance, long paragraphs typically do not entice readers to read.) Is the information the intended reader will look for readily accessible? Could it be more so? Are parts of the document (for instance, a return address or a date) obviously missing?

So much of the proofreading occurs up close that taking a brief, arm's length scan is the only way to uncover problems or opportunities you certainly won't notice otherwise, but that you can be sure readers will.

Again, no two proofreaders seem to have precisely the same approach—which probably means a single, flawless approach doesn't exist. In fact, I've asked dozens of proofreaders how they know they've caught everything.

Without a single exception, they've told me: you never do. It seems you cannot proofread enough or have enough people look at a document.

Discouraging? Perhaps. A more positive way to look at it, though, is to chalk it up to the wonders of our brain; the human brain is forever behaving in ways beyond our understanding and, seemingly, beyond our control. In Chapter 3 I'll discuss this phenomenon in more detail along with strategies you can use to better prepare your mind and your environment for proofreading.

3

To save time and effort, prepare to proofread

Success with just about any challenging task takes some form of preparation. Runners stretch first, speakers rehearse, physicians study X-rays, teachers create lesson plans. Even writers, to be most effective, prepare themselves to write through a series of activities called "prewriting" (more on that in Chapter 4). So it is with proofreading: To do it well you must first prepare.

Preparing to proofread involves more than just creating an environment free from distractions—although we'll talk about that too. The truth is, your biggest distraction in proofreading can be your own brain. Successful runners, speakers, physicians, teachers, and writers have learned that the brain can either work for or against them in accomplishing their goals. A runner worried about a previous knee injury probably won't perform at his best. The same is true with a speaker who's aware she isn't as prepared as she'd like to be.

Knowing a little more about how the brain works, then, particularly when we're wanting its help to proofread, can help turn a possible liability into a critical asset.

Preparing your mind

Gestalt psychologists were the first to discover that our minds tend to see things not as they are, but as our minds think they should be. The implications of this phenomenon for proofreading are enormous. Artist and author Carolyn Bloomer, in her book, *Principles of Visual Perception*, tells us:

> *This strong tendency of the mind to "correct" stimuli...explains why proofreading is a difficult task: Your mental "correcting" tends to tune out the very errors you are looking for. In one study the word "chack" was placed in two different contexts. In a sentence about poultry raising it was misread as "chick"; in a sentence about banking it was misread as "check."*

John P. Frisby, in *Seeing: Illusion, Brain, and Mind*, calls this tendency "conceptually driven processing," and he offers the following demonstration:

> *It's hard work digging clay.*
> *Save it for a rainy clay.*

Did you catch the difference in the last words of these sentence? If so, congratulations. Most people won't. Frisby's example makes another point as well: Proofreading handwritten text is even more dangerous than proofreading printed text.

Let's try a couple more. Read the next set of indented lines normally. What does it say?

> It was a once in
> in a lifetime opportunity.

Did you catch the repeated *in* in the first and second lines? Okay, try one more, another Frisby example:

UNIVERSITY
DRAMA STUDIO

SRING SEASON

1977

Give up? The *p* is missing from the word *spring*! Notice how variations in font size and type can also make proofreading more difficult. The addition of graphic or other visually stimulating elements to text can also complicate proofreading.

This problem of conceptually driven processing is compounded when we proofread our own work. Our brain also likes to protect our egos. Accepting the fact that we make mistakes at all is difficult. And our brain is the ultimate comforter. Just as we sometimes hear not what was said, but what might best serve us, we typically see what best protects our ego.

Clearly, the less you know or care about the context of a document, the better you can proofread it (another interesting distinction between good proofreading and good editing, which often is enhanced by knowledge about the subject). Here are some tips for mentally keeping a safe distance from the material to enable you to proofread more effectively:

♦ Avoid proofreading your own writing whenever possible.

♦ Find a buddy with whom to trade proofreading tasks.

♦ Take time away from your own writing if you must proofread it yourself—at least 15 minutes; 24 hours is best.

♦ Change your perspective by changing your proofreading environment—move to a different location, change chairs, or shift your chair to the opposite side of your desk.

♦ Print the document. A paper copy is easier to read than a computer screen and helps shift your perspective.

♦ Print the document in draft mode, which typically increases the space between the lines of text and hides formatting.

♦ Print a portrait (normally or vertically-oriented) document in landscape (or horizontal) mode.

♦ Print in a larger or less familiar font.(But choose a serif font, a font with the little "feet" such as the font you're reading now. Serif fonts, perhaps surprisingly, are easier to read.)

♦ Make sure the document is typed in a combination of uppercase and lowercase letters; all caps is both harder to read and more of an affront on the eyes.

♦ Work in small time increments—15-20 minutes at a time.

♦ Work only at your best times; the times in the day when you're most alert.

♦ Take regular breaks to stretch, rest your eyes, and mentally disengage from the task.

♦ Change to a totally different activity for awhile, especially when proofreading longer documents; return later when you're refreshed.

♦ Work to free your mind from internal distractions—emotional highs or lows, worry, preoccupation. (Make that phone call you'll be thinking about making anyway; vent your feelings by journaling for several minutes; have a good scream in a secluded location; or go outside and kick a tree. Do whatever works for you, but get rid of the internal noise. It probably won't leave on its own.)

Preparing your environment

According to proofreading expert Neita F. Geilker, Ph.D., effective proofreading takes more concentration than any other job, save that of air traffic controllers. (By the way, she, too, recommends breaks after every 20 minutes of proofreading simply because that's proven to be the effectiveness ratio for air traffic controllers.) A distraction-free environment, to the extent that's possible, is absolutely necessary.

Isolating yourself

Undoubtedly, your biggest hurdle here is people accustomed to having access to you. Here are a few tips perhaps you haven't tried yet for isolating yourself for concentrated work:

- Free yourself from the phone, even if it means trading favors with a co-worker.

- Let key people know you'll be unavailable *and for how long*. People tend to cut you slack if they know when they can reach you. Most urgencies can wait 20 minutes.

- If you don't have a human gatekeeper, create a voice mail or answering machine message to inform callers when you'll check for messages. Then keep that promise, and return calls promptly to keep your callers' trust.

- Close the door, and turn your back to any windows through which co-workers can make eye contact.

- If you don't have a door or real walls, leave your typical work space. Find some secret spot, even if it's an unused cubicle in another department. Let only one key person know your whereabouts.

- If you must, invent a meeting to escape to your spot.

- When a real urgency can't wait, stop right where you are. Return when you're able to re-focus.

Gathering key resources

The three key resources you'll need from time to time when you're proofreading are a dictionary, a grammar/punctuation guide, and a style guide. Let's take a look at each of these:

The dictionary. Of course, these help us with spelling and the occasional definition, but they also do some other pretty incredible things many of us long ago forgot about. Use a dictionary to check for word divisions (but I'd avoid these as often as possible to make reading easier), meanings of abbreviations and acronyms, tenses of irregular verbs, and irregular plurals of nouns.

Dictionaries also help out with the parts of speech of a word and its current usage. (For instance, *Webster's New World Dictionary* tells us that *impact* can be a verb as well as a noun, but as a verb it's considered colloquial: informal or conversational.) While you'll find some minor variations between dictionaries, they agree more often than not. Dictionaries continue to be the most up-to-date source of information on the constant changes in American English. To be truly useful, yours should be no more than 10 years old. Pick the one you find easiest to make your way around in.

If spelling is a challenge for you, take heart. As Mark Twain said, "Any imaginative person can certainly think of more than one way to spell a word." Check into phonetic spelling dictionaries available as books and pocket-sized computers. These "pocket cheaters" can even help you improve your spelling skills over time.

And what about those spell-checkers attached to most word processing programs? These are great—as quick-and-dirty tools go. I especially like Microsoft *Word 7.0*'s Automatic Spell Checking feature, which detects my spelling errors as I type the words! And that's not all: it automatically corrects common misspellings (*thier* for *their* and *teh* for *the*, for instance) all by itself! My point here is that tools to help you are available and becoming more helpful all the time. Use your software's spell-checking feature just before printing your paper copy for proofreading. But that's really the extent of these feature's usefulness. As I'm sure you're aware, spell-checking dictionaries are typically limited in scope, and they won't flag many problems that are, in fact, spelling errors (the *you* that should have been *your*, the *too* intended to be *to*, the *form* for *from*).

Grammar/punctuation guides. Even professional writers don't know all the rules; they keep one of these handy, and as a proofreader, you should too. I like *The Gregg Reference Manual,* which seems to be the most commonly used among the organizations I do business with, but other guides may be just as good. Pick one that gives you solid answers to the recurring problems you come across, and stick with it. Publishers release new editions of these books every few years, but you don't need the most current version. The information doesn't change that much.

Computerized grammar checkers, as I mentioned in Chapter 2, are generally not helpful. Especially when it comes to grammar issues such as active versus passive voice, the logic of these programs is sophisticated enough only to point out the possibility of a problem. For example, most grammar checkers will merely point out every instance in which you use the verb *to be*, one component of a passive construction. Not every use of the words *to be* is passive.

On the other hand, if you find a grammar checker that does help you, use it. Just stay away from grammar checking programs that merely alert you to possible problems without suggesting corrections. They can be big time-wasters.

Style guides. American English is not as black-and-white a language as we might hope. One reason our language is so difficult to manage is that we have a lot of latitude with issues of style, another printing term which in this case refers to the conventions followed by a particular organization, profession, or field with regard to these gray areas. Are department names and titles typically capitalized within your organization? Is the date on a letter centered or against the left margin? These are all aspects of your company's unique style.

If your company has developed such a style guide, it should be the style guide you use. Often these, if they exist at all, are stuffed in an executive secretary's drawer somewhere, and not officially "published." A second alternative is to keep your own file of letters, memos, reports, etc., written by respected individuals at your company. These documents are typically the safest unofficial models.

Whether you do a lot of proofreading or proofread only infrequently, a third alternative when it comes to handling style issues is to compile your own company-specific style guide, or list of conventions. Such a tool can really save you some time. If you do decide to put together such a guide, make sure you organize the guide in a way you'll find easy to refer back to. For instance, list all abbreviations together, all rules about spacing and proper format together, etc.

Lastly, consider using a style guide developed specifically for your field, industry, or profession. Magazines, newspapers, and many art departments, for example, use a style guide commonly recognized in that field, such as *The Associated Press Stylebook*.

Finally, if all else fails, a generic business writing style guide should do the trick. *The Gregg Reference Manual* (a grammar and punctuation reference) also includes such a style guide.

Making your work space distraction-free

Here are additional tips for making your concentrated work space productive:

- Clear your desk of all potential distractions.

- Find a work surface and chair where you'll be comfortable yet alert. With paper and pen in hand, that comfortable recliner at home might be tempting, but avoid it to stay alert.

- Use incandescent, not fluorescent, lights whenever possible, even if you must bring in a lamp from home. Fluorescent lights hum, flicker, and create glare, all of which distract and exhaust our hard-working brains.

- Have your resources within easy reach.

- Use a straightedge to guide your eye.

- Use a distinctly different color of ink: Your best bets (on white paper) are blue, green, or purple. Black ink, lighter colors, and pencil are too difficult to distinguish from your text; red causes many of us to recoil in memory of the marks our third-grade English teacher made.

Making it happen

To make sure you have the time and space planned for proofreading, a few additional tips might be helpful:

- Schedule times for proofreading, just as you would a meeting or appointment. Then keep the appointment!

- With larger projects or loose deadlines, set your own intermediate deadlines to avoid procrastinating.

- Explain the importance of solitude for getting your work done to those around you who may be sources of distraction.

♦ Take care of, or schedule in time for, other urgent priorities that, if left undone, may distract you. If I have a heavy proofreading task, I can find a million other emergencies to help me procrastinate. Scheduling these to be done at another time is sometimes the only way I can get myself focused enough to proofread.

I've devoted an entire chapter to preparing to proofread because it may very well be the most important factor in a proofreader's success. When you consider the mental preparation necessary to trust yourself to proofread, or for that matter, to accomplish any important task, I cannot emphasize enough the need to get yourself in a right frame of mind before you start. But let me leave you with the words of Maxwell Maltz, M.D., F.I.C.S., author of the important book *Psycho-Cybernetics*, who speaks of a universal truth about us all:

You are not your mistakes

Self-acceptance means...coming to terms with ourselves now, just as we are, with all our faults, weaknesses, shortcomings, errors, as well as our assets and strengths...Many people shy away from healthy self-acceptance because they insist upon identifying themselves with their mistakes...We must recognize our mistakes and shortcomings before we can correct them.

4

Before you proofread, edit

If you've ever attempted to paint an unprepared wall, you've no doubt learned a frustrating lesson. Taking the shortcut probably forced you to prepare the wall as you painted it, cutting into any time you might otherwise have saved. Perhaps the task even took longer than it would have had you taken all the right steps in the first place. And the final product may never have looked worth all the effort you put into it. The same is true of any document you attempt to proofread before it's been edited.

Many inexperienced writers try to produce a nearly final version of their document in essentially one attempt, believing in what a colleague of mine, Linda Comerford, calls "the myth of the perfect rough draft." First drafts are never truly ready for proofreading. In fact, writing experts tend to agree that to produce a well-written document, you should spend at least 50 percent of your total writing time rewriting or editing the document.

Try to disprove that theory. I'll admit, I myself have tried the edit-as-you-proofread (or worse, the painful edit-as-you-write) approach, typically on occasions when I've been in a real hurry. What inevitably results for me is a slipshod job of editing, and at least one zinger of an error always gets through. What tends to work best for most people is a writing process with four distinct stages.

The four stages of effective writing

Here is the process that works best for me with the approximate percentage of time I spend on each stage.

> ☞ **1. Prewriting (30%)**
> Prewriting is identifying and refining your document's purpose and your understanding of your reader's needs, then organizing your initial ideas into a general game plan.

> ☞ **2. Drafting (15%)**
> Drafting is actually writing the document. To draft effectively, write quickly, loosely following your game plan, seldom stopping to make changes.

> ☞ **3. Editing (50%)**
> Editing is clarifying, strengthening, and condensing the communication you attempted at the drafting stage.

> ☞ **4. Proofreading (5%)**
> Proofreading is polishing the final draft, ensuring that no errors in communication, however small or seemingly insignificant, make it through to the intended reader.

This is the basic writing process that the best university English departments have been teaching for at least the last 15 years. My students and business clients alike have found that handling almost any sizable writing task in these four distinct stages makes the writing work—with less effort and, believe it or not, even less total writing time.

Perhaps you were surprised that I—and others who make their living as writers—spend so much of our writing time editing. If you do not, perhaps it's because you do some of what I do at the editing stage under the guise of proofreading. Again, in my experience, combining stages doesn't work as effectively. Because editing is so often confused or otherwise combined with proofreading, it's worthy of more discussion here.

You may take a writing project from start to finish. In this case, the separate stages can seem indistinguishable. Or you may turn over your work at a particular point for someone else to edit or proofread. In the publishing field, different people (and typically several different people) handle the drafting, the editing, and the proofreading. Or you may work as someone else's editor and/or proofreader. Regardless of the division of labor in your writing projects, the tips in this chapter can help you get through the process efficiently and successfully.

For me, editing has three fundamental goals: clarifying, strengthening, and condensing the message drafted in the first stage. Let's take a careful look at each of these goals.

Editing goal 1: Clarifying the message

Cheryl Hamilton, in *Communicating for Results*, poses a significant question: "If no two individuals have the same frame of reference, how can a person ever communicate

100 percent effectively with anyone on any topic, even in the business setting?" She goes on to suggest that 100 percent communication, communication in which the intended message is understood absolutely as it was intended, probably never *ever* happens.

And with most forms of written communication you have just one chance to get the message across in the hopes it will be understood absolutely as you intend it. Add to this the fact that most people feel they're too busy to give careful attention to everything that crosses their desks and you'll realize that clarifying your thoughts is absolutely critical. Here are some questions I ask myself as I attempt to clarify my thoughts.

1. Is the purpose of my communication immediately apparent to my reader? Whether my purpose is to instruct, advise, demand action, provide information, or request a decision, my purpose should be immediately apparent to my reader. One of the most common errors I see business professionals make in their writing is that they fail to state the purpose of their letter, memo, report, or e-mail message right up front. Without this, the reader is left to guess at it and may lose patience and stop reading.

The best stage in which to catch this error in your writing is at the editing stage after your entire message has been drafted. In the typical draft of a letter or memo, the sentence stating the purpose of the communication, if it's there at all, shows up toward the end. If you're delivering bad news or trying to sell your reader on an idea he or she is not quite expecting, the end is where this statement belongs. In all other cases, however, it belongs up front, ideally as the very first or second sentence.

2. Have I made my message relevant to my reader? All too often I see writers focus on what they want their readers to know, not what the readers would most want or need to know. Especially in business communication, ignoring a topic's relevance to the reader could mean that the reader will ignore your message. At the very least, most readers will set the document or message aside in an electronic mailbox or the "I'll get around to it later" pile we all seem to have.

So at the editing stage make sure that you've made the relevance of your message clear by verifying that you've stated your purpose in a way the reader would care about. Instead of merely announcing a policy change and then starting in with the specific details, state—right up front—how your reader will be affected by the change. Don't save this information, vital to the reader, for the conclusion.

And don't be afraid to use personal pronouns, such as *I, we,* and especially *you* in most forms of business writing. Avoid expressions like *one, the individual,* or worst of all *this writer* or *this organization* in all types of communication, save perhaps the most academic. And while our English teachers discouraged us from using *you* in our writing, it can be one of your best tools for making the writing relevant to the reader's interests and needs. Here are a couple of examples of what I mean:

Avoid: This organization **has established a policy**...

Use: To better protect your interests as our customer, **we have established a policy**...

Avoid: Our **records indicate that** this service allows ...

Use: **Your telephone service enables you to**...

Challenge how well you've attended to your reader's needs with the "So what?" test. Could your reader have this response to your message after reading the first sentence? The second? The third? If so, your message may be in trouble.

3. Does each new thought make sense? Our English teachers called this concept paragraph unity. Each paragraph you write should be unified around one key idea. Don't try to tackle too much in one paragraph, or your reader may not get what you're trying to say.

One of the best tools at your disposal as an editor to ensure unity is the topic sentence. We all know what this is. A topic sentence is like a mini purpose statement for each paragraph; it's the one sentence in each paragraph that states the key idea of that paragraph. Topic sentences are critical guideposts for your reader, making absolutely clear—or as close to absolutely clear as possible—the salient message of each paragraph. If your paragraph is unified, every other sentence in it should support the topic sentence.

In the drafts of business communications I read, however, topic sentences are often missing. This happens because in drafting a document, the thoughts evolve as we write. As E. M. Forster reminded us, "How do I know what I think until I see what I say?" Through writing our thoughts become clear; naturally, when we're drafting, we may not be ready yet to think in topic sentences.

Insert missing topic sentences as you edit, preferably at the beginning of each paragraph. Your English teacher may have told you that anywhere in the paragraph is okay, but at the beginning of each paragraph is where they help your reader most.

4. Do my thoughts flow smoothly and logically throughout my document? Again, your primary concern should be whether the reader can follow your train of thought. Here I'm referring to the organization and coherence of your ideas. Part of what makes navigating your thoughts easier for the reader is the order in which you addressed things: Are your ideas organized in the way your reader would most likely expect or be able to follow them? Would your reader find the connections you've made between ideas easy or difficult to maneuver?

As an editor, look first for the overall organization of your ideas. Does it make sense? Would it make as much sense to your reader?

Next, make sure you've included other guideposts to help the reader, such as transitional expressions placed between sentences and paragraphs. At the beginning of this paragraph, for instance, I used the word *next* to help you make the transition from my last idea, organization, to this one. Did it help you out?

Here are some common expressions you might deliberately add in when you're editing to help readers make the transitions between your thoughts. Use such expressions liberally, but vary them or your readers might pay more attention to repetitive pattern than what you're trying to say.

Therefore	Consequently	As a result
Furthermore	In addition	In the same way
For example	For instance	In other words
However	On the other hand	In contrast
In fact	Above all	Most important
Also	As well as	What's more
First, second…	Next	Further
Finally	In conclusion	To summarize

Here's my final suggestion to help your thoughts flow smoothly and logically: Use words consistently. If in one paragraph, you refer to the folks you work with as *staff members*, continue to call them *staff members*. Yes, our English teachers told us repetition was bad, but if you shift in a later paragraph into calling them *employees*, then later *associates*, someone's likely to be confused. Plus, using the same words consistently builds coherence.

5. Are my thoughts clearly expressed? Here I must mention what many people feel should have been a four-letter word: grammar. Whether it's a favorite topic of yours or not, grammar is the device by which we construct the thoughts in our heads into verbal messages.

If just now the hair on the back of your neck started to stand up, relax. Believe it or not, most people have no trouble with most issues of grammar. Really! Where many people do get into trouble with grammar is with just five grammatical concepts. Think of these as five keys to clear communication:

1. Sentence structure
2. Subject-verb agreement
3. Active voice
4. Clear use of pronouns
5. Clear use of modifiers

Master these, and you'll have no difficulty editing your own, or anyone else's, written text. I'll cover the Five Keys only briefly. If any of them present a challenge for you, remember: Grammar rules are tools that, with practice, anyone can use effectively. For more extensive coverage on the rules of grammar, including practice exercises, check out *Better Grammar in 30 Minutes a Day,* by Constance Immel and Florence Sacks.

Key 1: Sentence structure

In one research study, U. S. executives identified poorly structured sentences (comma splices, run-ons, and sentence fragments) as a major "Ignorance Indicator" when dealing with other professionals. Not that there's really any connection between good grammar skills and intelligence. However, people do make the connection, so getting this grammar concept down is important to your image. The good news is that this is essentially an issue of punctuation. Compound and complex sentences (sentences containing more than one idea, or clause) should be punctuated correctly so readers clearly and easily understand your meaning.

Compound sentences. These sentences contain two independent clauses, which could in fact be two separate sentences. Here are the three correct ways to punctuate compound sentences:

1. Connect the two clauses with a comma plus a coordinate conjunction. For example:

> **Proofreading is important to catching**
>
> **embarrassing errors, but editing should**
>
> **always happen first.**

Coordinate conjunctions: for, and, nor, but, or, yet, so

---

2. Connect the two clauses with a semicolon. For example:

> **Proofreading is important to catching**
>
> **embarrassing errors; editing should always**
>
> **happen first.**

3. Use a transitional phrase or word (when used this way, called a conjunctive adverb) after the semicolon; follow it with comma. For example:

Proofreading is important to catching

embarrassing errors; however, editing

should always happen first.

> Conjunctive adverbs: consequently, however, therefore, furthermore, then, thus, nevertheless, moreover, indeed, in fact, of course, in addition, in brief

Complex sentences. Like compound sentences, complex sentences contain more than one idea, or clause. But in a complex sentence, one of the two ideas can't stand alone. The addition of one word, a "subordinating conjunction," makes one clause "dependent" on the other to complete the thought.

> Subordinating conjunctions: although, after, because, before, as, if, since, until, when, whereas, while, who, which, that

Here are the two correct ways to punctuate complex sentences.

1. Start with the dependent clause, the clause beginning with the subordinating conjunction, and put a comma between the clauses. For example:

Because **I always edit first, my documents**

are easier to proofread.

2. Start with the independent clause, and omit the comma between the clauses. For example:

My documents are easier to proofread

because I **always edit first.**

Key 2: Subject-verb agreement

Matching the right verb with a subject can be a trickier task than you might think. Multiple subjects, collective nouns, and intervening phrases can all confuse the match-up. Here are the basic rules:

♦ Singular subjects joined by *and* become plural.

The proposal and report are due by 5 p.m.

♦ Singular subjects joined by *or* stay singular.

Either a proposal or a **report must be**

submitted at the meeting.

♦ A combination of singular and plural subjects joined by *or* can be either singular or plural, depending on whichever occurs closer to the verb.

The proposal or these reports are my first

priority.

These reports or the proposal is my first

priority.

♦ Singular collective nouns (*group, team*) are singular.

The team determines **its next project.**

♦ *Everyone, everybody,* and *each* (when used as a pronoun) are singular.

When everyone is here, we can get started.

♦ Prepositional phrases often end up between subjects and their verbs. Take care that you don't let them confuse the subject-verb match up.

Each of the accounts has its own unique characteristics.

Key 3: Active vs. passive voice

I, like writing consultant Lorraine Seabrook, see writers failing to use the active voice more than almost any other writing difficulty. What is the active voice, and why is it important? Readers expect most sentences to follow a basic—and easily understandable—structure: subject (generally the doer of the action) + verb (the action) + object (the receiver of the action, if there is one). In an active voice sentence, the subject is, in fact, the doer of the action. Here's an example:

My manager complimented Jim for his innovative plan.

Manager, in the subject position, is the doer of the action. Compare this easily understood sentence with a second version, which attempts to convey the same idea:

Jim was complimented for his innovative plan by my manager.

With a passive sentence, your reader must wait until the end of the sentence to discover who did the action. Passive sentences communicate information in a convoluted, less personal, and more wordy way. Research has shown that:

- ◆ Active voice sentences are easier to understand.
- ◆ Active voice sentences are easier to remember.
- ◆ Active voice sentences require fewer words.

Notice, too, how easy it would have been to eliminate the doer of the action (my manager) from the sentence above altogether:

Jim was complimented for his innovative

plan.

Who complimented Jim? If your intent was to tactfully protect the identity of the giver of the compliment, then great; tactfulness is an appropriate use for passive voice. In fact, in the rare occasion when you must point out that someone is at fault, passive voice is much more effective than using *you* or naming the person by name.

Avoid: **Because you failed to return this**

form on time....

Use: **Because this form was not returned**

on time....

Avoid: **When John let Susan go last year....**

Use: **When Susan was let go (or left?) last**

year....

But in all other cases, write sentences in active voice.

> *Avoid:* **The plan was implemented.**
>
> *Avoid:* **The plan was implemented by our team.**
>
> *Use:* **Our team implemented the plan.**

Editing for active voice can be particularly challenging with technical material. Many writers of technical information confuse passive voice ("X was done") with objectivity. Stating ideas actively ("Y did X") can be just as objective and is generally more effective. Here are a few final examples, geared especially for more technical writing.

> *Avoid:* **From project specifications, it was determined that deflectors will be installed next month.**
>
> *Use:* **From project specifications, we determined that teams will install deflectors next month.**
>
> *Use:* **The project specifications indicate that teams will install deflectors next month.**

Key 4: Clear use of pronouns

Pronouns, those shortcut words we use to avoid repeating a noun, get many writers in trouble. To use pronouns effectively, these writers may need to tackle one of the three pronoun problems I see most often.

Noun-pronoun agreement. For the substitution of pronoun for noun to work, they need to agree in number: a singular noun needs a singular pronoun to replace it; a plural noun, a plural pronoun.

Avoid: **Everyone should meet** their **project deadlines.**

Use: **Everyone should meet** his or her **project deadlines.**

Use: All team members **should meet their project deadlines.**

Problems of pronoun case. A pronoun's case tells its reader whether it is acting as a subject in a sentence or being acted upon, as an object. Objects can be direct objects, indirect objects, or objects of prepositional phrases.

Avoid: **The issue was between Tim and** I.

Use: **The issue was between Tim and** me. (Object of a prepositional phrase)

Avoid: **If you have questions on this, call Sue or** myself.

Use: **If you have questions on this, call Sue or** me. (Direct Object)

Ambiguous pronouns. Naturally, for pronouns to work at all, they must refer back to a previously mentioned noun. Pronouns used ambiguously leave room for misinterpretation. Watch how you use these problematic pronouns:

this, that, these, which, it, they, them

If your pronoun does not clearly refer back to its noun, repeat the noun (or noun phrase) so there's no confusion.

Avoid: **If we need another test to confirm the analysis,** that **would not be a problem**....

Use: **If we need another test to confirm the analysis,** performing another test **would not be a problem.**

Key 5: Clear use of modifiers

Modifiers are adjectives and adverbs used to enhance the main idea(s) of a sentence. When used correctly, modifiers add vivid detail to aid a reader's understanding. When used incorrectly, they can distort the message. Modifiers can be single words or phrases. To use them correctly, place them near the word or words they modify.

Avoid: **To complete the report, you** only **need to total these figures.**

Use: **To complete the report, you need to total** only **these figures.**

Modifiers really create problems when the word or words they are intended to modify are missing from the sentence altogether.

Avoid: **As a valued customer, your call is important to us. (Is your call a valued customer?)**

Use: **As a valued customer, you are**
important to us.

Use: **Because you are a valued customer,**
your call is important to us.

Congratulations. You've made it through the five keys to clear communication (otherwise known as five common grammar pitfalls). Confidence with the tools of our language, including grammar, enhances your skills in clarifying, the first of your three goals in editing. Now let's move on to the second.

Editing goal 2: Strengthening the message

Many of us give little thought to how effectively our message is coming across to our reader. Is it really having the impact we'd like it to have? On the other hand, we've all read the lukewarm messages that, while they certainly get information across to us, don't really persuade us or entice us to act. In those cases, the writer probably didn't think much about the recipients of his or her communication. Otherwise, the writer might have made more of an appeal to our needs and interests.

A good editor looks beyond mechanics to aspects of writing that either weaken or strengthen the message. I typically focus on three basic issues when attempting to strengthen my writing: the completeness of my message, my use of words, and my tone. Let's look at these one at a time.

1. Is my message as complete as my reader would want or need? The approximate cost involved in sending any business letter out the door, including the writer's time, supplies, electricity to run the computer, etc. is—are you ready for this?—$100! If the reader must call you for additional information or explanation, that figure gets even higher. Anticipating all that your reader might want to know—note, I didn't say all you feel you should tell your reader—makes good business sense.

A communication is only as powerful as it is helpful *to the reader*. If, for example, you are sending out a letter regarding an upcoming meeting, here is the information you should include: time, date, or place a meeting is supposed to take place; an estimate of how long the meeting should last; a description of what attendees should bring to the meeting or be prepared to discuss; perhaps even an explanation for why those chosen to attend were chosen. To ensure the completeness of the information ask yourself, "What specific information would I need to know if I were the reader?"

Completeness is also accomplished through the use of concrete versus abstract, or clichéd, language. By *agenda items*, do you mean *pressing issues which may affect our relationship with a vendor*? By a *project's progress* do you mean *a status report on how established deadlines will be met*? Use language that is specific, descriptive, and meaningful to your readers. Otherwise, they won't see much value in reading what you write.

On the other hand, be careful not to overwhelm your readers with information they neither want nor need to know. Many writers have a difficult time separating their readers' desire to know from what they, as writers, want to tell them. Stop short of telling them all that's important *to you*. And have someone else read it to provide feedback on the relevance and amount of information you've included.

2. Are my words appropriate to communicate with this particular reader? Sometimes our words actually get in the way of our communication. Two years ago, my husband filed a small claims lawsuit (which he won, by the way) alleging that his former employer failed to pay a promised contribution to his retirement fund. This difficulty resulted in our first opportunity to deal with a local civil court system. A few weeks after he filed the suit, we received a nondescript letter from the county courthouse, which read:

> Notice of claim issued by
> sheriff returnable (date) at
> (time). Sheriff's service of
> process on Notice of Claim
> (sic) returned as leaving
> copy at the residence and
> mailing copy on (date).

How many times did you read it to get even a hint of what these folks were trying to tell us? Let me help: They were originally unable to serve the summons because the recipient was not home when the sheriff arrived. So the sheriff left a notice on his door and then mailed him a copy of the summons.

Which version would you rather read? Jargon, technical language specific to a particular company, field, or profession, often fails to communicate with anyone outside that company, field, or profession. At the very least, it alienates those of us "on the outside." I couldn't help but wonder how many people, attempting to deal with this local court system, had been discouraged, frustrated, or otherwise mistreated by this obvious lack of interest in true communication.

When we received the letter, my husband called the courthouse for clarification. And called. And called. And called. Do you suppose those folks were busy talking to other citizens who received similar letters? Now that's an expensive way to communicate! Eliminate the jargon from your language wherever you can.

If you're editing text with a lot of technical language unfamiliar to you, work with the writer (or another specialist in the area) to gain at least a minimal working knowledge of the content. If the intended readers of the document will likely be as thrown off by the language as you are, you may be in the perfect position to help the writer bring his or her language down to lay terms. People in highly technical fields often have this type of blind spot with regard to their readers.

The other type of language I work hard to eliminate when I edit is what I call archaic business-ese. You know what I mean, that language businesspeople often use when they're trying to sound impressive. Freelance editor and writer Helen O'Guinn sees this as one of the most prevalent problems in modern business writing; she calls it a "ghastly use of the English language," which instead of impressing, only demonstrates a writer's verbosity and self-importance. Perhaps "ghastly misuse" would be an even more accurate description.

Avoid expressions such as *per our last conversation* (when we last spoke), *in compliance with your request* (as you requested), *meets with your approval* (you approve), and *increase the effectiveness of* (improve). Substitute these archaic and wordy expressions, and hundreds like them, with common, simple, easy-to-understand language.

All good writing aims first to communicate, not impress. Institutional-sounding pseudo-business language seeks to impress first and, as a result, alienates. Use common language that all readers of your document will easily comprehend and likely respond to.

3. Is the tone I've established likely to get the response I want? In my 15 years experience as an editor and writing teacher, I've come to believe that we all have a style of communicating most comfortable to us. Some of us naturally gravitate to warm, personable ways of communicating. Others of us have little patience for what we consider flowery language and prefer to get right down to business. Still others feel the need to take a creative, even fun, approach to everything we write. And others prefer a less emotional approach: Stick to the facts and give plenty of them.

Whether your own personal approach is appropriate depends not only on the particular writing situation but also on the reader's own personal communication style. Write to suit the reader's style, rather than your own, to the extent that you can identify the style of your reader or readers.

If you cannot identify one or more readers' unique styles, a few general guidelines can serve almost as well:

♦ Never talk down to, or lecture, the reader. If you feel strongly about an issue, the least effective way to get a reader to see things from your perspective is to tell him or her what to think. Provide evidence; use your best emotional appeal, bring out the persuasive language. But never lose sight of the fact that your readers are equally intelligent, independent thinkers.

♦ Provide rationale to encourage a reader to accept an idea or take action. Flat out directives do not go over well with most adult readers. Be sure to explain the reason for any request you make. Rationale is especially important when you give a reader a deadline for response. For example:

To assist me in getting a quote to our prospect by Friday, please get the information to me by Wednesday.

♦ Always consider and include some statement of benefit to the reader. What would motivate a reader to read your communication? Why should he or she do what you're requesting? State a benefit from the reader's perspective—right up front for best results.

♦ Keep your tone as positive as you can. Don't overwhelm a reader with bad news; he or she won't read it. What good news can you include? Often the very same message can be communicated in a negative or positive manner. Choose the positive approach. For example:

Although we did not receive your resume by the deadline and therefore cannot consider it, we would be happy to review it during our next round of hiring.

♦ Never let anger or personal biases show. The more objectively you deal with someone, the more likely you are to get cooperation. Keep your communication objective and professional.

♦ Never demand or threaten. Even in the most difficult writing situation, for instance, a series of collection letters, your responsibility is to state facts and if appropriate, the possible consequences for inaction. But the reader should always be given an out, a choice that will help him or her avoid the consequences.

Editing goal 3: Condensing the message

Anyone who makes his or her living as a writer will tell you that good writing is concise writing. Regardless of how clear or powerful your message, it won't get read if you've taken too long to say it. Think about what you read as you thumb through your mail each day. Or your in-basket. Do you read everything that comes your way? If you're like most people, the answer is no. We're all busy, so we're all selective. We commit to reading documents whose purpose and relevance to us is immediately apparent and which look easy to read. If I have to read three long paragraphs before you tell me what you want from me, forget it. Chances are I won't read it. So your final, critical goal as an editor is condensing the message.

Readers like short words, short sentences, short paragraphs. The actual length of the word, sentence, or paragraph isn't as critical as whether they're easily readable. Most experts agree that an average of ten to 14 words is a readable sentence length. This does not mean that every sentence should stay within ten to 14 words; sentence variety is an aspect of sentences that entices a reader to keep reading. But on average, don't go excessively longer or shorter than that. Sentences covering highly technical information should be shorter because the words themselves may be more difficult.

As far as paragraph length, stay on the side of shorter paragraphs, especially in business writing, to encourage a reader to read. Nothing entices a reader to stay with you more than ample white space. Several concepts we've already discussed (using active voice and avoiding archaic business language) have the added advantage of condensing the text. Here are a few additional tips that, if you practice using them, will help you out-edit many professional editors!

Use strong verbs. More than any other part of speech, verbs carry the strength of your message. The verbs you pick will either express your ideas concisely and powerfully, or weaken and belabor your message. Pick your verbs carefully.

Avoid: **There** are **two reasons why this approach** is **the one we should pursue.**

Use: **I (or "We" or "The team")** should pursue **this approach for two reasons.**

Avoid: **These results** are important to consider **because they show...**

Use: **These results** indicate... **(That they indicate something important should be obvious.)**

Reduce clauses to phrases and phrases to words. Our language gives us an endless variety of ways to say the same thing. Concise writing never uses a clause when a phrase will do, or a phrase when a single word can get the same message across.

Avoid: **The account that contains the error is mine.**

Better: **The account with the error is mine.**

Best: **The faulty account is mine.**

Turn noun phrases into verbs. "Nominalizations" are noun phrases less effective writers use in place of strong verbs. Use the verb form instead!

Avoid: **The department has** made a recommendation **to...**

Use: **The department** recommended...

Avoid: **The president** will make an announcement **about...**

Use: **The president** will announce...

Avoid overusing sentence "warm-ups." When we're speaking aloud, we often use sentence "warm-ups" that provide just the instant we need to figure out what we want to say. But we can weed most of these out of our written language. The two most commonly used warm-ups, also called "expletives" begin with the words *it* and *there*. Almost invariably, weeding out the warm-ups results in a better sentence.

Avoid: It is important that **we start the meeting on time.**

Use: Let's **start the meeting on time.**

Avoid: There are **several important reasons for the change.**

Use: The change is **important for several reasons.**

Reduce unnecessary words and phrases. If you want your report read, reduce the number of words in it! The three keys mentioned so far will all help you reduce unnecessary words. See what else you can eliminate or rephrase in the sentences below. (Doing this well takes practice!)

> *Avoid:* **Please permit me to take a moment of your time to inform you that there are many issues it is important that you consider before a recommendation is made by you as to the one best solution to the problem that we've been discussing.**

> *Use:* **Please consider many issues before recommending a solution.**

Editing well takes practice, and editing skills, when practiced, continue to evolve. If editing is a new endeavor for you, be patient with yourself. Take one or two of the strategies I've presented in this chapter and practice using them until you see your skills improve. Then build your repertoire with new strategies.

Editing is never a perfect science. Different editors tend to focus on different strategies for improving text. All are productive efforts if ultimately the message a writer intended comes closer to the message a reader receives.

5

Proofreaders' marks

Marking errors on a document can be a complicated process, especially if someone else must make changes from your marks. Most documents simply don't provide a lot of extra white space in which to write extensive directions or explanations. And unless you're a writing instructor trying to educate as you proofread, you don't need to write instructions or explanations. You can use symbols to indicate necessary changes. Any consistently used and understood marking system can get the job done, but I recommend turning again to professional proofreaders, who will willingly loan us their set of widely-recognized proofreaders' marks.

Using the marks the pros use can make communicating with someone else easier. The pros' marks are logical representations of what you would want to communicate (insert this, delete that), and they're fairly straightforward, so you can quickly educate an uninformed author of your marking system, saving you both time. These marks are also widely published, so your writer may already may be familiar with them. Finally, if someone ever questions your credibility as an editor, using the official proofreaders' marks might also gain you some credibility. But always make sure you and your writer have a common understanding of the marks you'll be using.

Even if you edit and proofread strictly for yourself, taking the time to learn these symbols can save you time and help eliminate those frustrating moments when, on returning to your document to make changes, you have no idea what your markings mean.

One final note: Proofreaders' marks are fairly standard among the professionals, but subtle differences in how they're used and occasional differences even in the marks themselves, do exist. No two lists of proofreaders' marks are identical. I'll mention the variations, as they're relevant, but my fundamental goal is to offer you a standardized, widely recognizable set of tools you'll find easy to use. These magic marks appear on pages 73-75. Before we get into how best to use them, let's review a few fundamental tips for good proofreading:

♦ Proofread on paper rather than on screen.

♦ Give yourself room to work; print your document in draft mode or otherwise increase the space between the lines.

♦ Run the document through a computer spell-checker before you start proofreading; don't waste time finding easy spelling errors. If you don't have an electronic version of the document, have the writer or editor do this for you.

♦ Print with wider margins, if possible, in case you need room for an elaborate explanation or query. (We'll discuss queries later in the chapter.)

♦ Look back over your proofreaders' marks. Are *they* correct? Will they make sense to someone else?

Common proofreaders' marks

Mark	Meaning	Example
ℯ	Delete word, character, or punctuation	When does she really need it?
ℯ	Delete and close space	occassion
stet...	Stet (undelete)	It went very well.
∧	Insert word or character	What is the time?
∧ or ∨	Insert most punctuation	Sue's big old desk
:⊗	Insert colon	the following:
=∧	Insert hyphen	world famous
⁻∧ or ⏐M	Insert dash (em dash)	home at last
⏐M	Change hyphen to em dash	home at last
⏐N	Change hyphen to en dash	1970 1979
⊙ or Ⓧ	Insert period	That desk is heavy.

Mark	Meaning	Example
/	Replace word, character, or punctuation	due ~~today~~ by 5 p.m. *Friday*
‿	Close space	th e team
⌢	Reduce space	his right arm
#	Insert space	his left arm
∽	Transpose word, character or punctuation	use the word best
⟲	Move as shown	only gave her a dollar
move from ...	Insert extensive text	take this advice. move f pg.
move to ...	Move extensive text	My advice is ... move t pg.
	Insert page break	— — — —
¶	Start new paragraph	Another point about...
no ¶ or ∿	No new paragraph	Another point about... *or* Another point about... This is an example
less space (	Reduce space vertically	My office downtown may be moving.
# >	Insert space vertically	When will you know for sure?
ss (	Single space	My office downtown may be moving.

Mark	Meaning	Example
ds (	Double space	ls (When will you know for sure?
⌐	Move right	$ 30,000 ⌐
⌐	Move left	⌐ Take it to heart
‖	Align text	‖ Tom Phillips / Liz Hannah / Sid Allen
≡ or cap	Capitalize	Washington, d.c.
lc.	Make lower case	Post Office
SP	Spell out	3 times last year
	Add underline	Stages in the Writing Process
underline		1. Prewriting underline / 2. Drafting / 3. Editing / 4. Proofreading
no underline	Remove underline	Stages in the Writing Process no underline
		1. Prewriting / 2. Drafting / 3. Editing / 4. Proofreading
ital BF no BF	Add italics, boldface	ital Time magazine / He said nine pieces BF
	Remove italics, boldface	He said nine pieces no BF

Tips for using proofreaders' marks

Using any new set of tools well takes training and practice, so the rest of this chapter is devoted to providing just that. Complete the exercises throughout the chapter, and I guarantee you'll feel more confident using these marks when we're finished. Let's get started with some basic ground rules:

- ◆ While standardized marks are certainly a help, marking changes effectively requires good common sense. Never squeeze too much information into a small space! Your marks are useless if the author can't read them.

- ◆ Cursive writing is fine so long as others can read it. If your handwriting is hard to read, print. However, some letters, especially when used singly, are easier to read one way or the other. Use the easier-to-read version; print *i*'s, *m*'s and *n*'s, for instance, but use cursive for *l*'s and *r*'s.

- ◆ Use the simplest marking you can to correct the error. For instance, if several letters are missing from a long word, don't simply insert each letter; replace the entire word:

  Avoid: **admin̬stratif̬decisions**

  Use: ~~**adminstratif**~~ administrative **decisions**

- ◆ Marginal notes are always an option. Circle marginal notes that are instructional or explanatory to distinguish them from actual changes.

♦ Don't waste time repeatedly correcting errors that a computer's global search and replace feature can do instead. If you won't be making the actual corrections, note global changes at the top of the document.

♦ Don't play mind-reader; if you're not sure about what the author intended, query the author. Usually this is done with a circled marginal note.

13 The meeting will be held this Tuesday, the 12th, at noon.

Q: Monday is the 12th. Is this what you meant to say?

Deleting words, characters, or punctuation

Deletions are probably the easiest marks to make. Crossing out text comes quite naturally for most of us. But the trick to doing this well as a proofreader is to mark the deletion so that the material you want deleted can still be seen. The best mark for this purpose may be unfamiliar to you, but it's quite simple to use. The basic mark, useful for deleting a single character or punctuation mark, is an upward slash ending at the top with a loop.

plain English

To delete an entire word or several words, run the mark horizontally, still ending it with a loop.

Plain English words work!

The loop at the top of the slash helps to make the mark more noticeable. Especially when you're deleting only part of a word, the deletion loop helps make clear where the deletion stops.

She seemed disinterested in the

presentation.

To delete several sentences or an entire section of text, circle it, put an *x* through it, and add your deletion loop to the circle in a clearly visible spot, for instance, a margin.

One topic we will discuss at the staff meeting is lateness. Many staff members are reporting to work from five to fifteen minutes late. What can we do to solve this recurring problem?

Deleting and closing space

To delete a letter in the middle of a word (or a number in a grouping of numbers), indicate that both the character should be deleted and the resulting space closed up by marking the deletion normally and then putting arching lines above and below the deletion.

writting skills   **$100,000.00**

Marking to close up space is necessary only within a word or set of numbers. If you eliminate entire words or letters from the beginning or end of a word, closing up the space between words is assumed. Simply mark the deletion.

please re̶consider

considerin̶g̶ the time

Practice deleting words, characters, and punctuation

Delete every incorrect word, character, and punctuation mark you see in the sentences below. My solutions appear in the Appendix.

1. We never do anyanything well till we
   cease to thingk aboutt the mannern the
   manner of doing it.

   —William Hazlitt

2. The easiest) person, to deceive is one's'
   own self.

   —Edward Bulwer-Lytton

Undeleting words, characters, or punctuation (stet)

There's an easy way to indicate you've changed your mind about a deletion (or, let's be honest, you screwed up) and that material you've marked for deletion or change should be left as is. It's called a stet mark, and it's simply a series of dots beneath the material you've deleted or changed.

My staff is e̶x̶t̶r̶e̶m̶e̶l̶y̶ excited about the
move.

Use as many dots as you need to identify the correction. If the correction is small or you doubt the dots will be visible enough, remember you can always make a circled marginal note.

Now they're all vying for the best office

space.

Inserting words or characters

Inserting words and characters into text may look tricky, but it really isn't. Insert an up-pointing arrow, also known as a caret, at the base of the line precisely where you want the addition to go, and then add a character or word above the line of text.

He who hesitates is lost.

He hesitates is lost.

You typically don't need to indicate the need to add obvious spaces (as around the word *who* in the previous example). Occasionally, however, you may want to make the spacing clear by adding close-up hooks:

Plan his garden before you till it.

Without close-up hooks here, your change could result in *plant his* instead of *plan this*. If your additions are longer or may get confused with another addition nearby, use a bracket, and tie the bracketed set of words to the caret.

A fool and money parted.

—Anonymous

If your addition is longer than can comfortably fit above the line of text, use a bracket, and move it to the margin, again tying the words to the caret.

It was the worst of times.

best of times, it was the

—Charles Dickens

If your addition is extensive (and won't easily fit in the margin), consider referring the author to another spot for the changes. See "Inserting extensive text" on page 93. Inserting several letters in the same word or several numbers in a segment of numbers can be confusing. A better option is to replace the entire word.

Avoid: Honluu

Use: ~~Honluu~~ Honolulu

More information on replacing follows the next set of exercises.

Practice inserting words and characters

Try your hand at inserting missing words and characters in the following sentences. My solutions appear in the Appendix.

1. To be, or no to be, tha is question.

—William Shakespeare

2. Correct ths seres of numbers:
   18 19 20 2 22 23 4 25

3. Early to bed and makes wealthy, and
   wise.

—Ben Franklin

4. The occasional errr is tool for edcaton.

Inserting punctuation

Insert punctuation just as you would a character, with a caret. Use the standard, upward-pointing caret to insert punctuation that goes at the base of a line (periods, commas); use a downward-pointing caret to insert punctuation above the line (apostrophes, quotes).

Tom the security guard yelled Stop thief

Because the period is the punctuation mark hardest to see, you have a couple of other options to indicate the addition of a period. Instead of using the caret, enclose the period in a circle, or enclose an *x* in a circle to represent a period.

Poor Tom was having a bad day⊙

or

Poor Tom was having a bad day ⊗

Colons, too, can be difficult to see, so insert one by enclosing it in a circle and using a caret to indicate where the colon should go.

We like these treats cookies, candy, and
cake.

To insert a hyphen, use a caret and two short, stacked lines (since one line alone would be easy to miss).

It was a time̿‸honored tradition.

A dash is two hyphens with no space between them and can be indicated in one of two ways. Use a caret and two short lines side by side, or insert this symbol: $\frac{1}{M}$. To change a hyphen to a dash or to insert a dash, use either of these two symbols:

We were finally home‸at last!

or

We were finally home‸at last!

We were finally home‗at last!

Indicate the need for an en dash (used to separate groups of numbers) by inserting this symbol: $\frac{1}{N}$. Use this symbol to change a hyphen to an en dash or to insert an en dash.

1970‗1979

If your markings could in any way be misunderstood, support your proofreaders' marks with a circled, marginal comment.

Mark the wall 10ˇfrom the door.

(use symbol for "feet")

Practice inserting punctuation

Insert missing punctuation in the following sentences. The answers appear in the Appendix.

1. He used a hammer nails and glue to repair Eds window

2. Wasnt the memo sent to Sandy
   president Pete vice president and Larry
   treasurer

3. Bring two items to class a notebook and
   a pen

4. Ed will like the state of the art look of
   his new window

5. Remember these symbols of the 60s tie
   dyed shirts and peace signs oh, what
   memories

6. Hank was in school during these years
   1980 1985

Replacing words, characters, and punctuation

When you need to replace, rather than merely insert or delete material, the classic advice, "Keep it simple" couldn't be more important. To mark out single characters or punctuation, use a slash without the deletion loop. Then write the correction as clearly as you can above the line of text. Note the caret for the insertion is also not needed.

I really enjoy proofreading.

To replace an entire word, cross straight though the word, just as you did with a deletion, but again, leave off the loop.

Proofreading well really takes ~~praktise.~~ practice.

Note that in this last example I could have individually replaced the letter *k* with a *c*, and the *s* with a *c*, but doing so would have made the replacement more difficult, not only to mark but to read afterwards. Remember, keep it simple.

Avoid the temptation to mark directly on top of existing text, especially punctuation. Even with a distinctive color of ink, your marks are easy to miss when they're written in the line of text. As with words and characters, slash through punctuation errors and write in corrections above the line. But if putting the new mark above the line could cause confusion—a comma confused for an apostrophe, for instance—go with a caret at the base of the line.

As pay raises go, I prefer Tom's, not John's.

Practice replacing words, characters, and punctuation

Replace every incorrect word, character, and punctuation mark you see in the sentences below. If insertions and deletions work better, use those instead. The answers appear in the Appendix.

1. Gud punktuation skills are important to good proophreading.

2. Commas; not semicollons enclose unnecessarie phrases.

3. Where theirs marriage with love. there will be love without marage.

—Ben Franklin

4. Pair a dice is were I am,

—Voltaire

Closing space

Indicate that extra space in a line of text should be completely closed up with close-up hooks, or arching lines above and below the space to be closed up.

Sam lost his favorite note book.

Note that these are the same marks you use along with the deletion mark when you want to both delete something and close up the resulting space, as within a word or set of numbers.

writing skills   **$ 100,000.00**

Small close-up hooks are often helpful when an insertion makes the surrounding spacing unclear.

Plan his garden before you till it.

Reducing space

To indicate that space should be reduced between words but not closed up entirely, use only the top close-up hook.

All the great speakers were   bad speakers

at first.

—Ralph Waldo Emerson

If you delete either entire words or letters from the beginning or end of a word, closing up the space between the words is assumed. Do not use the close-up hook.

Plain ~~English~~ words work!

please ~~re~~consider

considering the time

To reduce space between lines of text, see the section on inserting and reducing space vertically on page 96.

Inserting space

To insert space in a line, insert a caret at the base of the line where the space should be, and above the line, indicate space with a # sign.

carryover

The # sign is widely used to indicate "space" by professionals in publishing, English writing education, and other fields. Of course, others recognize this symbol to mean "lb." or "number," so be sure your author knows ahead of time how you're using it.

To insert space between lines of text, see the section on inserting and reducing space vertically on page 96.

Practice closing, reducing, and inserting space

Insert, reduce, or close space as needed in the sentences below. Delete or insert characters also as needed. My solutions appear in the Appendix.

1. Too err is humman, to for give divine.

—Alexander Pope

2. Writting isn't sohard; no harder than
   ditch- digging.

   —Patrick Dennis

3. The plan his friend gave him grewtoo
   tall.

4. Ifonly computers could proof read!

Transposing words, characters, or punctuation

Many proofreading errors are the result of transposed, or switched, words or characters. Sometimes the simplest mark for correcting this type of error is an s-shaped line connecting the transposed items.

Good is good not where better is expected.

—Thomas Fuller

Transposing is merely another way of replacing an error. In the example above, I could have replaced the error instead (using a slash and writing the correction above the error), but transposing helps save both you and anyone actually making the changes some time.

Transpositions work, however, only when they are easy to read. If the s-shaped mark crowds the text, making it difficult to read, replacing may be the better option.

Avoid: **Good is not good where better is**
expected.

Use: **Good is not good where better-si— is**
expected.

Also avoid using transposing if the transposed items are far apart from each other or your correction would require multiple transpositions. These situations result in overly complicated corrections. Correct by replacing instead.

Avoid: **Well said is better than well done**

Use: **Well ~~said~~ is better than well ~~done.~~**

> —Benjamin Franklin

Avoid: **Never confuse wiht motion action.**

Use: **Never confuse ~~wiht motion~~ action.**

> —Ernest Hemingway

Be careful to clearly identify where punctuation should go when it's near a transposition. If space is limited and punctuation becomes hidden by your marks, replace instead or clarify where punctuation should go with a note.

Avoid: **We can do no great things—only small things with great loev.**

> —Mother Theresa

Use: **We can do no great things—only small things with great ~~loev.~~**

Use: **We can do no great things—only small things with great loev.** OK

Avoid transposing numbers. Too many of us misread numbers too easily. Replace an entire segment of numbers instead.

Avoid: **555-4879**

Use: **555-~~4879~~** 4789

Practice transposing words, characters, and punctuation

Transpose any needed words, characters, and punctuation in the sentences below. If replacing works better, replace instead. The answers appear in the Appendix.

1. **Laugh yourself at first, before anyone eles can.**

    —Elsa Maxwell

2. **Learning is a which will treasure follow its owner everywher.e**

    —Chinese proverb

3. **A money and his fool are soon partde.**

    —61st century saying

4. **We can lessons draw from the past, but cannot we live in it.**

    —B. Lyndon Johnson

Moving as shown

To indicate that a word, words, or an entire segment of text belongs in a different place, carefully circle it, and use an arrow (attached to the circle) to indicate where it should be moved.

> The constituent, pleading her case (tirelessly), remained standing as everyone left the room.

Be careful to clearly identify where punctuation should go when it's near a "move as shown" mark. If space is limited and punctuation becomes hidden by your marks, clarify where punctuation should go with a note.

> Adults can buy tickets (as well as children) ok

When editing, move entire paragraphs, or parts of paragraphs, to a different location on the same page by using the same approach. Be sure you've circled all the text you want moved, including punctuation; and use the arrow to indicate clearly where you want it to go.

> The world is moved along, not only by the mighty shoves of its heroes, but also by the aggregate of the tiny pushes of each honest worker. I long to accomplish a great and noble task, but it is my chief duty to accomplish humble tasks as though they were great and noble.
>
> —Helen Keller

If your move changes your paragraphing in any way, be sure to include the appropriate paragraph mark.

John's presentation went on entirely too
long. Many of those attending the seminar
seemed bored with his topic after the first
ten minutes. Someone should help John
understand that most people won't listen to
long speeches, especially when the content
is only remotely relevant. I believe it was
George Jessel who said, "If you haven't
struck oil in five minutes, stop boring."

For more information on marking changes in paragraphing, see the section on starting new paragraphs on
page 95.

Moving text to or from a different page is slightly more
complicated than moving text on the same page. See
"Inserting extensive text" on page 93.

Practice deleting, inserting, replacing, transposing, and moving text

Use the proofreading techniques we've discussed to correct the problems in the sentences below. Remember also
to add and remove space as needed. The answers appear in
the Appendix.

1. Itis a mistake to look too far head Only
   one link in teh chaan of destiny can be
   handled at a time.

   —Winston Churchill

2. This tiem, lik all tiimez is a veryvery good
   one, if know we what todo with it.

   —Ralph Waldo Emerson

3. Time is dead as long as is being it
   clicked off by little hweels'; only when
   the clock stopps does timem come too
   life?

   —William Faulkner

4. Jack of all none and master trades.

   —Maria Edgeworth

Inserting extensive text

When editing, moving extensive amounts of text from one page to another is a two-step process. First, circle the text to be moved to another page, and place a circled reference note as close as possible to this circled text.

> Last year's earnings were, unfortunately, lower than we had anticipated...

move to pg. 26

Your note should always include the page number you want the text moved to.

Second, on the page where the text is going, place another circled reference note as close as possible to where you want it to go. If space is limited, a caret tied to the reference note can help to clearly indicate the point at which the new text should be inserted.

> John's presentation focused on two topics: a report on last year's earnings and a projection of next year's earnings. Future earnings look very promising...

move from pg. 25

This second reference note should include the page number the text is coming from. Always double check to make sure your "move to" and "move from" references correspond. If the text to be moved is multiple paragraphs long, perhaps occurring on multiple pages, circle all the text to be moved and label it, typically with a capital letter inside the circle (or each separate circle if text is on multiple pages).

Text to be moved

Both your "move to" and your "move from" notes should refer to the letter you've assigned the text. Again, always double check to make sure your "move to" and "move from" references correspond.

Last year's profits were, unfortunately, lower than we had expected.

Some rather major expenses we had not expected took a big bite out of our profits.

Next year, however, will be different. We have made some changes in production and shipping procedures that we expect will boost our sales and profits.

A

move A to pg 27

Destination of moved text

When making several moves like this in the same document, use consecutive letters (A, B, C, etc.) so there's no confusion about what goes where.

If shifting your text between pages changes paragraphing in any way, be sure to include the appropriate paragraph mark. For more information on marking changes in paragraphing, see the section on starting new paragraphs on page 95.

John's presentation focused on two topics, a
report on last year's profits and a projection
of next year's profits. Future profits look
very promising....

Starting new paragraphs

To indicate that a new paragraph should be started,
use a symbol that looks like a backwards *P* with two legs.
Place this mark directly in the text where the paragraph
break should occur or, if the mark could be missed, in the
margin attached to a caret indicating the precise breaking
point.

There were many influential people present
at the annual gathering. Among them were
the presidents of Acme Manufacturing as
well as our own CEO, John Smith. Last
year the gathering was held in Tahiti;
however, this year we decided it would be
more logical to have it at a more accessible
location.

To remove a paragraph break, use the same symbol
with *no* in front of it. Again place the symbol either directly
in the text or in the margin with a caret.

There were many influential people
present at the annual gathering.

Among them were the presidents of
Acme Manufacturing as well as our own
CEO, John Smith.

An alternative way to indicate no paragraph break is
demonstrated on the next page. Be careful to make this

mark vertically so it can't be confused with the transposition mark.

> **There were many influential people present at the annual gathering.** **Among them were the presidents of Acme Manufacturing as well as our own CEO, John Smith.**

Inserting and reducing space vertically

To indicate the need for more or less space between lines of text, you have a couple of options. Choose your option based on how specifically you want to indicate the amount of space to be inserted or removed.

The less specific option is to put a # sign in the margin where you want the space increased and use a sideways-pointing caret to indicate the specific spot.

> **# Better to remain silent and be thought a fool**
> **than to speak out and remove all doubt.**
>
> —Abraham Lincoln

To reduce the space between lines of text in a less specific way, bracket the lines of text you want closer together, and make a circled marginal note.

> **less # Better to remain silent and be thought a**
>
> **fool than to speak out and remove all**
> **doubt.**

A second, more specific way to indicate the precise amount of space you want inserted is to use a two-letter symbol in the margin: *ds* for "double space" or *ts* for "triple space." To specify where you want the double or triple space to occur, bracket the lines of text you want separated with more space.

ds (
 Better to remain silent and be thought a

 fool than to speak out and remove all

 doubt.

—Abraham Lincoln

To leave precisely one line's worth of space between two lines of text, bracket the lines of text, and in the margin, use the two-letter symbol for "single space": *ss*.

ss (
 Better to remain silent and be thought a

 fool than to speak out and remove all

 doubt.

Moving text horizontally

Sometimes text may appear indented too far to the right or not indented enough (too far to the left). Of course, this can result from a paragraphing problem; if so, use the paragraph marks described earlier. But when the problem is one of alignment, not paragraphing, use an expandable bracket to indicate the correction.

A bracket "pointing" to the right indicates "move text to the right"; a bracket pointing left indicates "move text left." Whichever direction you go, align the vertical leg of the bracket with other text to indicate how far you want the text moved.

Move left: Move right:

   Tom   Tom

   Phil   Phil

   ⌐————⌐ Bill Bill⌐

   Sue   Sue

Several lines of text can be shifted at a time in this way. Widen the bracket (up and down) to include all the lines you need to move. Note, too, that the bracket can be placed on either side of the text. Choose the side that most clearly indicates how far you want the text moved.

Avoid:

    ♦ **Read the document slowly.**

    ♦ **Read the document aloud.**

    ♦ **Read the document backward**

Use:

    ♦ **Read the document slowly.**

    ♦ **Read the document aloud.**

    ♦ **Read the document backwards.**

If the text were right justified (with the text at the right margin aligned), the "move right" bracket would be more appropriately placed to the right, not the left, of the text.

Aligning text

An easy way to correct several lines of text misaligned in both directions is to place a double vertical line next to the text. This mark does not indicate exactly where the text should line up, only that it should be lined up vertically.

Tom Johnson
Phil Smith
   Bill Roberts
Sue Wilson
  Jill Jones
Bob Thompson

Aligning text is often necessary with columns of numbers. But aligning numbers typically requires more precision, so you may want to use this align symbol in another way. If your numbers should be lined up by decimals, for example, run a single vertical line down through the column of numbers, waving the line to align the decimal points.

```
1,289 05
1,400 50
  400 75    ( align
  500 46      decimals )
  768 80
1,050 78
```

Because this line running through the text could easily be missed, adding a marginal note is also a good idea.

Capitalizing text

To indicate that a single, lower-case letter should be capitalized, either underline the letter with three small lines or circle the letter and attaching the circled note *cap* above the line of text. Whichever symbol you use, use it consistently.

state street

valentine's day

To capitalize an entire word, an acronym, a group of words, or even an entire line of text (as in a header or for emphasis), you have two options. Which is clearer depends on how much you have to underline as well as surrounding punctuation.

ymca — all caps

He shouted, "Hold that line!"

Making text lower case

Turn a capital letter into lower case by placing a single slash through it and attaching the circled note *lc* above the line of text.

Community College

Chris Hankinson, President

To make an entire word, an abbreviation, a group of words, or even an entire line of capitalized text lower case, circle the text, and attach an *all lc* note.

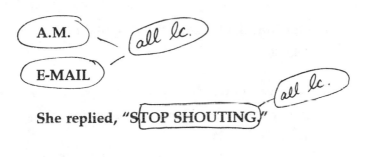

Spelling out text

Proofreaders often must indicate that an abbreviation or other word short-cut should be spelled out, typically to conform with either a company-specific writing style or standard business practice. The numbers one through ten, for instance, are normally spelled out in a business letter, as are dates, most contractions, abbreviations, and acronyms (especially when first used in a document).

To indicate that text should be spelled out, circle the text, and attach the circled note *sp*.

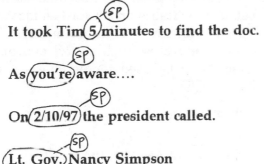

Practice capitalizing, making lower case, and spelling out

Capitalize, make lower case, and spell out as needed in the sentences below. The answers appear in the Appendix.

1. Our president signed the Proposal on
   1/12/96.

2. Dear mr. jones:
   Please accept my Dept.'s apology for the
   error.

3. Please keep this pin Confidential in Fla.,
   La., or Ga.

4. John's promotion in january was
   delayed until tues.

Adding and removing italics, boldface, and underlining

To indicate that text should appear in a special font,
such as italics or boldface, circle the text, and attach the
appropriate label: *ital* for italics or *BF* for boldface. Italics
are most often used to indicate book and magazine titles
and words refered to as words (such as *ital* above). Both
italics and boldface may be used for emphasis, as in a
header.

(Newsweek) magazine   *ital*

Please write (Do Not Bend) on the envelope.   *ital*

(Ten Ways to Stop Crime)   *BF*

To remove boldface or italics from text, circle the text,
and again attach the appropriate label: *no ital* for no italics
or *no BF* for no boldface.

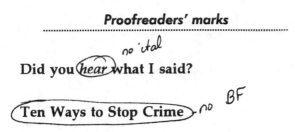

Did you *hear* what I said? — no ital

Ten Ways to Stop Crime — no BF

Underlining is most commonly recognized as another way to communicate italics; before computers made applying italics easy, we indicated italics with our typewriters by underlining. Because it is often confused with italics, actual underlining should be used sparingly.

To indicate actual underlining, your best bet is to circle the text you want underlined, and attach the circled note *underline*.

Ten Ways to Stop Crime — underline

To remove underlining from text, circle the text, and attach the circled note *no underline*.

Ten Ways to Stop Crime — no underline

Putting it all together

Use the proofreading techniques we've discussed to correct the problems in the sentences below. Remember also to add and remove space as needed. The answers appear in Appendix.

1. I cant right 5 words but that I chang seven.

   —Dorothy Parker

2. Did you know the italian word ciao *literally* means I am yur slave

3. Only an mediocre writter always at his best.

    —W. Somerset Maugham

4. Our blunderz mostly comefrom leting our wisshs intrepret our dutys.

    —Anonymous

5. Their is nothin final about mistake, except it's being take as fnial.

    —Phyllis Bottome

6. if you wuld notbe forgotten, as soon as you are dead and rotten , either write thinks worth readding, do or things worth the writting.

    —Benjamin Franklin

If proofreaders' marks were unfamiliar to you when you started this chapter, be patient with yourself as you begin to use them. As with anything else, the marks become easier to use with time, practice, and patience. You may want to keep the Proofreaders' Marks chart (from the beginning of the chapter) close at hand until the marks become second nature to you. If you do much proofreading and can appreciate how dramatically proofreaders' marks can help cut your proofreading time, trust me, you'll use them, and they *will* become second nature.

Finally, if you proofread for others, remember to let your authors in on your new set of shortcuts; otherwise, they'll be of limited use to you. But take the time to educate your authors, even if all you can do is show them the list of marks. This will enhance your effectiveness and may also strengthen your writing partnership with your authors.

6

Proofreading step by step

Let's face it, proofreading takes time most of us feel we never have enough of. Particularly if you've taken time to edit a document—to clarify, strengthen, and condense your message—proofreading may seem like just one more time-consuming task. Perhaps proofreading even seems super-fluous to you after editing. You may wonder, "Surely I've caught everything; what could be left to find after all that editing?"

While you no doubt found some glaring typos and the like while editing, you weren't proofreading. So, you probably did not catch everything. Proofreading and editing require two fundamentally different conceptual processes. Editing is a process of analyzing and resynthesizing conceptual chunks of information into coherent and effectively expressed ideas. Its ultimate goal is to form a coherent and meaningful whole. Editing requires viewing the forest, not the trees.

Proofreading, on the other hand, requires viewing the trees—and the branches, the leaves, and even the bugs on the leaves. It requires repeatedly separating the components of language from any meaning so the brain doesn't insist on allowing us to see what we want to see.

Proofreading is the last task in pulling together any meaningful *and error-free* piece of writing. The trick, however, is tackling this last stage in the writing process as efficiently as possible. This chapter will help you get the most bang for your proofreading buck by helping you focus on those errors that matter the most and errors you're most likely to find.

The most critical errors

While we'd like to catch every single mistake in our writing, missing some types of errors can be more detrimental than missing others. Mistakes that miscommunicate in a way that results in embarrassing, costly, or even dangerous situations absolutely must be eliminated.

Some types of documents, just by their nature, must be perfect. Some examples include:

♦ Instructional materials describing procedures which, if mishandled, could be dangerous.

♦ Safety manuals.

♦ Physicians' orders on charts or prescriptions.

♦ Engineers' or architects' blueprints.

♦ Pilots' flight plans.

♦ Records documenting utility pathways, such as underground gas lines.

You may be able to identify documents used in your field or profession in which complete accuracy is critical. Failure to effectively proofread these documents can be catastrophic.

Even documents in which a mistake would not result in a risk to life or limb, a failure to proofread can carry heavy financial or other consequences. At the very least, a mistake could prove embarrassing. Some examples of this type of document are:

♦ Business proposals and bids promising goods or services for a specific price.

♦ Legal contracts and letters of agreement.

♦ Materials to be professionally published.

♦ Materials to be mass produced or otherwise mass distributed (as over the airwaves or computer networks).

♦ Form letters.

♦ Executive summaries of important reports.

♦ Reports or journal articles on controversial or ground-breaking topics.

♦ Correspondence intended for important or potential clients.

♦ Job applications, resumes, and cover letters.

In this time of regular and erratic job changes, correspondence intended for a potential employer can make or break your success in the search for a job. Especially now, in an employment market flooded with solid candidates in many fields, employers often reject candidates solely on the basis of a single typo on a job application, resume, or cover letter. Fair? Perhaps not. Reality? You bet.

Other professionals choosing the self-employment route can quickly learn how detrimental a simple typo can be in certain types of documents. A self-employed friend of mine recently found himself in quite a position when he discovered that two numbers transposed in a bid for services ($3,500 for $5,300) had committed him to completing work for $1,800 less than he intended to bid. Most small businesses can't afford too many of those kinds of mistakes.

And specific kinds of errors tend to get noticed more than others, regardless of the type of document. Misspell someone's name, for instance, and trust me, he or she will notice. Sure, some readers are more forgiving than others, but if that first impression is critical, or you'd really like a reader's unquestioning cooperation on an issue, get the name right.

And if you're writing to a more analytical reader, you'd better get those facts, figures, and all the little details right. To these readers, a simple typo suggests a general lack of competence. Again, fair? No. Reality? You bet.

Other types of errors the typical reader is most likely to notice include:

- Misspelled or otherwise incorrect organization, program, or project names.

- Incorrect dates.

- Incorrect figures, especially when they involve money.

- Misordered sequences (numerical or alphabetical).

- Incorrect page numbers in a table of contents.

- Material including specific details or highly technical information.

- Funny—and often embarrassing—errors resulting from wrong words, transposed letters, or grammatical problems (such as unclear pronoun references).

- Missing chunks from a sentence.

- Missing format elements, such as the return address or a signature missing from a business letter.

- Misaligned columns.

- Mistakes occurring in headlines or headers.

- Mistakes on a title page or in a first line or a first paragraph.

- Mistakes in captions or other short segments of text surrounded by white space.

Shortcuts to save you time

There's no foolproof shortcut to proofreading quickly and well, but a few key strategies can help save you time.

- Always make sure the document has been spell-checked.

  Even if the writer or editor has likely run the document through a computerized spell-checker, always ask. (Could someone have made changes and forgotten to recheck the spelling?)

- Proofread on paper, not on screen.

  If you receive the document on disk or on line, don't try to proofread it there. While electronically cutting and pasting your changes might seem a way to save time, every proofreader I've ever talked to agrees that you'll catch more errors more quickly proofreading it on paper.

♦ Make sure you know what's expected of you.

As a proofreader you may at times find yourself in a situation in which a document's owner insists that he or she can't afford the time you really need to do your job perfectly. "Fix only the glaring errors," he may tell you, or she'll say, "Don't make major changes at this point, or we'll never make the deadline." While you may not feel comfortable proofreading under these circumstances, there will be times when you have to accept these limitations in deference to the document's owner. Chapter 9 offers more suggestions for working with others as a proofreader.

♦ Gain some distance from familiar material.

If the document is yours or you're otherwise familiar with its content, remember to gain some distance from it before you proofread (or even edit) it. Doing so will improve both your effectiveness and your speed.

♦ Finally, do all you can to create an environment conducive to proofreading.

Distractions of all varieties, as we discussed in Chapter 3, will rob you of more time than will any other single factor. Separate yourself from those distractions, and you'll save energy, frustration, and time.

Remember the experts' approach

Chapter 2 suggested a five-step proofreading approach to help improve your odds of catching everything. Here again is that process:

1. Read the entire document, or a good-sized chunk of a larger document, through once slowly, reading for overall content and meaning.

   If you've just edited the document, this step probably won't be necessary. You know what it's about. But if the writer or someone else provided the editing and you'll be doing the proofreading, start here because some proofreading decisions you'll make will require having an overall sense of what the document is about.

2. Read the document through even more slowly, this time *aloud* and correcting all errors you find.

   You'll catch most proofreading errors at this stage, including errors an editor may have missed: errors of grammar, missing text, some spelling errors, some punctuation, duplicate words, and some wrong words altogether.

3. Read the document a third time, silently or aloud, focusing especially on trouble spots.

   Focusing on the errors most of us commonly make—and miss—is the goal of this third step. Nothing can help speed a process along more than knowing what you're looking for. So at this step, you'll want to focus on the areas of a document where problems tend to occur most, areas where readers notice errors most, areas especially challenging for most proofreaders, and areas where your author may have particular problems.

4. Read the document backwards.

   Reading backwards can be tedious, and some (including myself) consider it torturous. It is the single best way, however, to catch some kinds of spelling errors and other hard-to-catch errors, such as transposed numbers.

5. Scan the document at arm's length.

   To catch glaring errors of format (for instance, misaligned columns, misnumbered sequences, spacing or margin problems, or missing elements such as a date), scan the document one final time. With this last step, adding format elements such as headers and additional white space offers the additional advantage of making the document easier and more enticing to read.

To help you get the most from the time you spend proofreading, the rest of this chapter focuses on the types of errors you should attempt to catch at each step of the process and the best ways to catch those errors.

Step 1: Read for overall content and meaning

Provided the document has had some solid editing, you probably won't be changing a lot of text at the proofreading stage. However, sometimes a second or third pair of eyes can catch even an editing problem that someone else missed, say a confusing passage or an overly technical use of language. As the proofreader, especially if you've never seen the document before, you may be in the best possible position to point out even big problems—if you start with a broad perspective.

Don't waste your time "painting the wall" when the wall may still need repair. In other words, read the overall document first, and consider these questions:

♦ Does it make sense to you?

♦ Would it make sense to its recipient?

♦ Does its tone seem appropriate?

♦ Does it flow logically from one idea to the next?

♦ Is its purpose expressed clearly and early?

♦ Does it seem to meet its author's objectives?

Circle any problems or questions you have as you read, but don't make any specific markings at this point. Then pose those problems or questions to the editor or author. Many times someone expected to proofread hesitates to ask those "stupid" questions, especially after several others have reviewed a document. But I have been impressed at the number of times someone completely uninvolved in putting a document together raises issues that seem like sheer brilliance to the rest of us caught up in viewing the "forest." Trust your judgment, and ask those gut-level questions. You may save everyone some time and embarrassment.

Gaining the big-picture perspective before marking changes also ultimately helps you to proofread more effectively. Whenever I fail to take this advice and dive right away into the minute details of a document, I often make knee-jerk corrections which I can—and sometimes do— change my mind about once I get further into a document, a paragraph, or even a sentence. But if I discipline myself to read an entire document (or large chunk of a long document) before marking anything, I not only save time, but I focus on finding the right errors throughout the rest of the proofreading process.

Step 2: Reread the document, slowly and aloud

The benefits of reading a document aloud cannot be overstated. No technique does more to help you catch almost everything!

If you haven't tried this technique, I know what you may be thinking. You haven't read aloud to yourself since elementary school. Perhaps you even remember a second- or third-grade teacher who encouraged you to grow into reading silently and maybe even told you that reading aloud wasn't appropriate for anyone over age eight. And, yes, in your current work environment, if your co-workers heard you reading aloud, they may think you're losing your mind.

But all this aside, *try it. It works.*

Find an isolated spot (which, as suggested earlier, is a good idea anyway); then get used to hearing your own voice become a reading tool once again.

Finding the embarassing grammar errors

Reading aloud can help you catch errors related to *all five* of the grammar concepts I called the Five Keys to Clear Communication in Chapter 4. Of course, you hope the editor already caught these problems (especially if that editor was you), but if the editor missed something, reading aloud is your best hope of catching the error now.

These errors can prove embarrassing in two ways. First, writers confident with grammar often equate some grammar problems with a lack of intelligence (though, again, there's no real relation). Second, often when you think you're saying one thing but your reader understands something else, chances are, a grammar problem is to blame. These blind spots in our communication can prove especially embarrassing.

While reading aloud will help you catch these problems, knowing how to fix grammar errors can be equally challenging. For immediate help, look back to Chapter 4. Then if you'd like a more extensive brush up on the rules of grammar, look into *Better Grammar in 30 Minutes a Day,* by Constance Immel and Florence Sacks.

Here again are the Five Keys to Clear Communication and tips for catching the error by reading aloud. Each key is followed by an example of how a problem related to that grammatical concept could prove embarrassing if you let it get by you. Throughout this section, I've used proofreaders' marks to make the needed grammar changes.

1. **Sentence structure:** properly structuring compound and complex sentences. Improper sentence structure results in comma splices and run-ons, which fail to signal to your reader a coming change in thought.

Example:

> **Catching grammar errors is the editor's task**
>
> **when the editor misses something it**
>
> **becomes the proofreader's error to catch!**

Correction:

> **Catching grammar errors is the editor's task,)**
>
> **when the editor misses something it**
>
> **becomes the proofreader's error to catch!**

Reading aloud helps you chunk information into cohesive ideas. If, while reading a single sentence aloud, you suddenly feel plunged into a completely different thought, take a closer look: Was the signal (proper punctuation) there?

2. **Subject-verb agreement:** matching singular verbs to singular subjects and plural verbs to plural subjects.

Example:

> **None of the assistants proofread well.**

Correction:

> **None of the assistants proofread well.**

Reading aloud can help you detect problems with subject-verb agreement, but only if you're listening for the right thing. In fact, trusting your ear can be tricky when it comes to picking the right verb. In the example above, for instance, the subject is *none*, not *assistants*. (Think of *none* as meaning *not one*.) Listen for subjects, and the verbs usually come along just fine.

3. **Active voice:** stating ideas in a direct and concise, subject + verb + object, fashion.

Example:

> **Sue was recognized by the team.**

Correction:

> The team
> **Sue was recognized by the team.** Sue

Listen (and watch) for two specific aspects of language when attempting to detect passive voice. First, passive voice requires some form of the verb *to be*. Above, the past form of *to be, was* must be added to the root verb *recognized* to make it a passive verb.

The second aspect is even easier to listen for because it typically occurs at the ends of passive sentences: a prepositional phrase starting with *by* (though in this case the *by* phrase is not essential to create a passive sentence: *Sue was recognized* is also passive).

4. **Clear use of pronouns:** using pronouns that agree in number (singular or plural) and are clearly matched with their antecedents; also using subject pronouns as subjects and object pronouns as objects.

   Avoid: **The company should stand behind** their **policies.**

   Use: **The company should stand behind** its **policies.**

   Company *is singular, so* its *is the proper pronoun.*

   Avoid: They **say that playing with fire is dangerous.**

   They *is an ambiguous pronoun. Who are* they?

   Use: Fire experts **say that playing with fire is dangerous.**

Example:

> **Bring your proofread document to Sharon or myself.**

Correction:

> **Bring your proofread document to Sharon or ~~myself~~.** me.
>
> Me *is the object version of the pronoun, and in this case it's an object of the preposition* to.

Here again, your ear can be a big help in catching these kinds of errors, but only when you know what you're looking for. Occasionally one of these, especially when said out loud, zings even the most ungrammatically astute ear.

5. **Clear use of modifiers:** using modifying words and phrases to enhance rather than distort an idea.

Example:

> **My goal was never to be famous.**
>
> *This is not what this radio talk show interviewee intended to say!*

Correction:

> **My goal was never to be famous.**
>
> *What she really meant: she was famous, but she'd never tried to be.*

These, too, are often less visible on the page than audible to the ear. And the best ones are the funniest ones. Note, though, that if the misplaced modifier is yours, you still may not hear it. This is another good reason to get others to help you proofread your own work. If you get others to help you proofread—other people hear it immediately. Then you'll hear them laughing.

Finding omissions

Reading aloud can also help with the single most common type of proofreading error: omissions.

Missing words. If you're reading aloud carefully, you'll pick up immediately on word omissions. They'll probably cause you to stumble. Watch particularly for omissions of small words, such as *is*, *in*, or *if*, when the word following is *it*.

Missing text. Rereading aloud will also help you pick up on missing segments of a sentence or even missing parts of a paragraph. These types of errors happen often when someone has been directly copying text from one document to another, as happens in comparison proofreading. (Comparison proofreading is more fully described in Chapter 2.) Often if a particular phrase is repeated in the document being copied, the typist can look away for just a moment and then inadvertently skip to the next occurrence of the phrase, missing an entire segment of text in between.

Missing negatives. Also, if you're reading aloud, you're more likely to pick up missing negatives, such as *no*, *not*, and *never* as well as negative prefixes and suffixes, such as *un-* as in *uninteresting* and *-n't* as in *don't*, *won't* and the like. These can be particularly confusing or embarrassing. If they're not caught they can make the opposite point the writer intended!

Missing letters. Finding missing letters in words is more of a challenge. Of course, spell-checkers will catch the omissions that don't happen to create other words. But plenty of omissions do just that. For these, again, read aloud, and you'll certainly stumble over most missing letters and hopefully those that could really be embarrassing if you had missed them. A participant in a writing workshop I taught recently shared an experience she had in which an outraged customer, obviously attempting to intimidate, wrote to her demanding that his concern be taken to the "Director of Pubic Relations"! Amazing what effect leaving out one skinny, little *l* can have. In this case, the workshop participant proceeded to call an executive secretary she thought needed a good laugh and inquired as to where she should direct this fine gentleman's inquiry.

Missing punctuation. Punctuation marks occurring within a word, typically apostrophes and hyphens, are also very commonly left out. Two of the most often omitted marks of punctuation in the English language are, in fact, apostrophes and hyphens, perhaps because punctuation imbedded within a word is easier to miss. While many readers may forgive the occasional innocuous missing hyphen or apostrophe, some missing marks can't help but call attention to themselves—the apostrophe in *he'll* for instance.

But, fortunately, most of these are problems you can hear, *especially* when the so-easy-to-make error creates a completely different word. Spell-checkers won't catch the problem, but you'll hear it!

For those few remaining letter and punctuation omissions that neither spell-checking nor reading aloud will catch (for instance, hyphens missing from compound words), you may have better luck reading the document backwards. Obviously, no single technique guarantees that you'll catch everything. But using this several-step, multiple-strategy process will increase your odds of finding even the toughest-to-find omission errors.

Finding duplications

Duplicate words. Duplicate words occur most typically at the end of a line of text, from one line to the next, and in strings of small words, such as *So be it as it may*. But thanks to spell-checking software, which also calls our attention to adjacent duplicate words, detecting these is less of a problem.

Duplicate letters. Duplicate letters, too, generally fall within the domain of spell-checkers, except of course for those duplicate letters which create other words. (For instance, duplicate *t*'s make *cuter* become *cutter*.) Again, reading aloud will help with most, if not all, of these.

Extra words. Duplicate words that don't happen to appear next to each other and other stray words left in where they don't belong—these remain a problem, even for our spell-checkers. But (you guessed it) reading aloud should also help you catch these.

Any still-leery-to-read-aloud proofreaders out there: Are you convinced yet to give it a try?

Catching wrong words—butt knot awl weighs

Now, reading aloud won't help you catch the use of a wrong word if you're unclear about the meanings of easily confused words to begin with (*affect* for *effect*, *imply* for *infer*, etc.). For those my best advice is to study a style guide, such as *The Gregg Reference Manual*, which contains an extremely useful section called "Word Usage."

But for word mix-ups you'd recognize, reading aloud, once again, can help. That's a good thing, too, because word differences our spell-checkers won't catch that result from single-letter errors are fairly common.

Transposed letters and other near misses. Imagine the potential embarrassment you could face if you mistakenly transposed two letters and *marital* became *martial* (no ball-and-chain jokes, please), or if the first name of your most important client, *Brian,* appeared in a letter as *Brain.* Beware those near misses that turn out to be other words. *Really* for *ready, than* for *then,* or *than* for *that—* these are yet more examples of how artful our brains are at letting us see what we want to see. Reading aloud carefully and slowly is, once again, our only hope for convincing our brains we want to see errors.

Word derivatives. Word derivatives often aren't detected by a spell-checker either. For example, a *chose* for a *choose* may slip by a first silent reading. Another problem area is with suffixes: *forms* or *former* for *formed.* Even though your spell-checker won't catch *product* for *produce* or *manufacture* for *manufacturer,* you most likely will when you're reading aloud.

Small words. The same is true for small words often substituted for others when our brains once again insist on seeing things not as they are, but as they ought to be: *an* for *and, you* for *your* (two of my own personal favorites), *in* for *on, by* for *be, to* for *the,* and *or* for *of*…. You get the picture.

Homonyms. Finally, let's not forget the homonyms. These are words that, alas, sound alike but have different meanings. Classic homonym errors often involve confusing possessive pronouns: *it's* for *its, there* for *their,* and *your* for *you're,* for instance. One workshop participant of mine had an excellent proofreading suggestion. When contractions are involved (these are word shortcuts using an apostrophe, such as *I'm* for *I am*), read every contraction as the two separate words it's made from: read *it's* as *it is*. Doing so helps ensure that the word truly should be a contraction, needing an apostrophe, and not a possessive pronoun, none of which takes an apostrophe.

Other homonym errors take careful reading to catch—along with a fairly solid knowledge of word differences. *Site*, *cite*, and *sight*, for instance, are three very different words. (*Site* refers to a place, such as a construction site; to *cite* means to refer to or quote; *sight* has to do with vision or a view.) Unfortunately, unless you use a word often in a particular context, you may not even be aware you're confusing one word for another.

And sometimes you may still be misusing the word! Many people confuse the words *principle* and *principal*, for instance; and if they work in a financial field, that's a problem! (*Principal*, not *principle*, refers to the capital sum of money that draws interest.) At the very least, be sure you're using the words common to your profession or industry (or the profession or industry you typically proofread for) correctly.

Reading a lot and studying word differences are ways you can build your knowledge of word differences over time. Again, I recommend using a reputable style guide, such as *The Gregg Reference Manual*, which typically contains an elaborate listing of homonyms and other words that sound so similar they, too, are often confused (words such as *eligible* and *illegible* or *perimeter* and *parameter*).

Catching troublesome punctuation errors

Because catching punctuation errors is so critical a part of good proofreading, Chapter 7 is devoted to helping you address the toughest errors most writers make. Proofreaders who know what errors are most common can be the most effective in catching them. These are the errors you'll most likely catch by reading aloud at Step 2, rereading the document slowly and aloud. You could argue that Step 2 is the most important proofreading step simply because you'll catch most errors then. Busy business professionals often consider a document proofread after Step 2.

So should you continue with Step 3? The answer to that question depends on how important catching all the errors is to you, the writer, your boss, her boss.... Unfortunately, quite a few types of errors can and do slip by even when we're reading aloud. I've mentioned many of these above.

Step 3: Focus on the trouble spots

The good news about Step 3 is that it involves selective proofreading. You typically won't re-read the entire document. The goal of Step 3 is to focus on the trouble spots:

♦ Where mistakes most often occur.

♦ Where the writer typically has difficulty and reading aloud won't catch every error.

♦ Where you may tend to assume there are no errors.

♦ Where the reader is most likely to notice the errors.

♦ Where the information *must* contain no errors.

Whether you read aloud or silently is your choice. But I'll say it again: There's no substitute for reading aloud. When something I'm writing must be absolutely right, I go back to these key areas and re-read them aloud.

Typical problem areas

Where problems typically occur. Mistakes of all kinds tend to occur at the beginnings, and especially the endings of things: chapters, sections, pages, lines, tables.... Beware especially the bottom of a page, section, or chapter, because as writers start to wrap up their thoughts, they tend to make more errors.

Where proofreaders miss errors. You, too, may tend to miss more errors as you're beginning or ending a proofreading session. Even brief breaks from proofreading, while necessary, can lead you to miss errors you would otherwise catch. And where you find one, look for others. Many proofreaders have found that errors tend to "nest" together. Perhaps this phenomenon occurs because writers tend to make errors close together; a more likely explanation, first posed to me by freelance editor and writer Helen O'Guinn, is that once you, as the proofreader, catch an error, you may be less likely to look for another one very nearby. So take another look!

The trouble with numbers. Numbers tend to give both writers and proofreaders a great deal of difficulty. Many proofreaders have told me they struggle, to some extent, with "a mild form of dyslexia" when it comes to numbers. Whether they appear in dates, quantities, dollar amounts, columns of figures, or elsewhere, numbers deserve another look. But you may want to wait until Step 4, which calls for reading the document backwards. Sometimes reading numbers backwards is the only way to catch an error.

An individual writer's problems

A particular writer's tendencies for errors, if you know what these are, should also guide your attention through

Step 3. Whether they're problems with grammar, punctuation, capitalization, spelling, or even typing habits, knowing as much as you can about who you're editing for can make this step go faster. Chapter 9 discusses specific suggestions for finding out and documenting these tendencies. Doing so can be another time-saver.

Grammar and punctuation problems. Does the writer have difficulty with particular grammar or punctuation problems? Reading aloud will have helped you catch most grammar problems and some punctuation problems. At Step 3, double-check for the errors you may have missed, especially those you know the writer struggles with, such as an abundance of commas, a lack of apostrophes, comma splices or run-ons, sentence fragments, or passive voice. If your writer has a prevalent problem or host of problems, yes, you may be re-checking the entire document. If he or she needs that much help, you'd better recheck the document anyway. But be strategic: Look for just particular types of problems

Capitalization problems. If your writer has difficulty with conventions of capitalization, reading aloud won't help you catch these errors, so take another look. If you're a little rusty yourself on the rules of capitalization, review them in a style guide (ideally one published by your organization or industry; but if that's not available, you know by now that my preference is *The Gregg Reference Manual*).

More common capitalization problems involve differences in the rules based on different communication contexts. Within an organization, for instance, you may be expected to capitalize such things as department names and positions (the Accounting Department, Manager). When writing outside the organization, as when you're writing to a customer, these are never capitalized. Only proper nouns, that is, one-of-a-kind persons, places, things, or concepts, are capitalized.

Spelling problems. These, like problems with numbers, are not most effectively handled at Step 3. Those not easy to catch with the help of a spell-checker followed by reading the document aloud can probably only be caught by reading the document backwards in the next step. Find more tips on proofreading for spelling errors there.

Trouble where you assume there is none

Proofreading well involves a constant willingness to challenge even the most obvious. When I proofread for myself, I invariably find a zinger of an error: a date with the wrong year, the misspelling of a long-time client's name or organization name, *p.m.* versus *a.m.* on the time sent line of a fax, a zip code off by one digit (*217* versus *317*), mention of four key points when I really have five. Beware the areas of a document where you least expect an error to crop up. Especially when the document is your own, take a second look at even the most obvious information.

And because some of the most offensive errors result from misspelling a reader's name, organization name, or the name of some special project he or she cares about, get into the habit of collecting documents that verify information and spellings. These include:

♦ Business cards.

♦ Corporate literature.

♦ Corporate directories.

♦ Minutes from meetings mentioning special projects.

♦ Names of receptionists and secretaries you can tactfully call when all else fails.

Most important, *always* verify this information at Step 3. You might always think to verify a *Klein* versus a *Kline*, but discipline yourself to check even when it's a name typically spelled a certain way. Are you sure it's *Smith*? It could be *Smyth*! Are you sure that the word *Company* or *Co.* or *Inc.* shouldn't be included as part of the name? Are you sure the right words have been capitalized? Does the name need a trademark or service mark? (For more information on trademarks or service marks, see another book in this series, *Copyright Plain and Simple* by Cheryl Besenjak.)

Here's the bottom line: The minute you assume you've got a name completely right, chances are pretty good you'll make some small error that won't feel so small to a reader, and that reader (an important client, for instance) won't ever mention it. I've made errors like this—typically with clients I know very well—and not discovered my error *for years*. So be careful.

Trouble a reader will likely notice

At the beginning of this chapter, I listed types of errors readers are most likely to notice. In addition to noticing these types of errors, readers tend to pay more attention to certain places in a document than they do others. Errors made in those areas rarely get by them.

In a nutshell, readers most notice text that is either nearest large areas of white space or that looks different. The beginnings and endings of paragraphs, sections, and especially entire documents, tend to get the most attention from readers. Writing experts agree that the two most important parts of a document, based on the attention readers pay to them, are the first and last sentences, in that order. First sentences make the first impression; final sentences leave the lasting impression.

Other text surrounded by white space also gets more attention from a reader. Bulleted lists of points make more of an impression than a full paragraph containing the same information. Columns of text or numbers, charts, or any visual element surrounded by white space will also get special attention. (Want to stress a key point? Do it in a one-sentence paragraph. It will get noticed.)

So use caution when proofreading these parts of a document, and be leery, as well, when you're proofing any text formatted differently: headlines, text in boldface or italics, any text that looks different from the norm. All these will get more attention from a reader. Unfortunately, text that looks different in some way is also more challenging to proofread! So these areas, too, are worth another look.

Trouble where there should be no trouble

Also at the beginning of this chapter, I listed examples of documents in which any error at all could prove disastrous. While most of us don't have the lives of others in our hands with every document we write, we all write certain documents or document sections that *must* be right. As a self-employed business professional, my proposals, which include proposed budgets, must be flawless. An error there could cost me embarrassment, my credibility—or worse.

In the same vein, double check the accuracy of scientific, technical, or foreign language in highly technical or persuasive material. A mistake there can blow your or your author's credibility instantly.

Any important document or important section of a document demands a Step 3 (Focus on the trouble spots) read through even if you think that it's right.

Step 4: Read the document backwards

By this point, the document should be just about there. In fact, you may feel that you don't need to complete Step 4. As I've admitted, I often don't. But as much as I hate to say it, this fourth step, reading the document backwards, is necessary when the document must be flawless. Spell-checkers, reading aloud, and double-checking trouble spots may still allow you to miss a few key types of errors.

Reading a document backwards isn't really reading it at all. Instead you're looking at each individual letter, moving your eyes slowly backwards across a line, perhaps even following the line with an index finger, never "seeing" more than a single word at a time—which is exactly the point of this step. Some types of errors are so elusive that only this tedious analytical activity can free the mind from seeing what it wants to see, from over-interpreting, and from making connections that aren't really there.

What types of errors am I talking about? Fortunately, there are just a few:

♦ Spelling errors that neither spell-checking nor reading aloud may catch.

♦ Other spelling errors and duplications of words if a computer spell-checker is not available to you.

♦ Harder-to-catch punctuation and spacing errors.

♦ Transposed numbers and other number errors!

♦ Other special problems you may choose to focus on.

Tough spelling errors

Reading a document backwards gives you one more edge in catching every spelling error, especially those you haven't caught by this point. While reading backwards is no more likely to catch certain types of errors than the other spell-checking techniques we've discussed (homonyms, for instance, are still spelled correctly however you're looking at them), the discipline of reading backwards, I've found, does help me to catch just about everything. For instance, reading backwards may encourage you to take that second look at the spelling of proper names you might not have questioned. I even tend to double check capitalization when I'm reading backwards.

If that miracle invention, the spell-checker, is not available to you, or if you don't have a document in an electronic format, reading backwards is more critical. Otherwise, you may not see those harder to catch errors: tiny duplications or omissions that don't really affect pronunciation, duplicate words at the ends of lines or from one line to the next, and types of spelling problems you may not be aware *you* suffer from. (As I'm typing this, for instance, I keep misspelling *omission* as *ommission*.) If I didn't have the benefit of a spell-checker, I *would* take the time to read backwards.

Tough punctuation errors

Reading backwards always helps me with missing or misplaced apostrophes, especially in plural possessives, and compound words in need of hyphens. Because these are imbedded between words and pronunciation often gives no hint they should be there, reading backwards is a surer way to catch problems with these marks, the two writers most often leave out.

As far as other types of punctuation problems, reading backwards doesn't help much. Most punctuation found outside an actual word requires reading the context in which it's found to discover any problems. I do discover missing partners in paired punctuation (quotes and parentheses, for instance) when I'm reading backwards as well as punctuation mistakenly italicized, underlined, or put in boldface along words appearing next to them.

And one other thing I almost always discover when reading backwards is extra spacing before or after punctuation or between words. Now that's careful proofreading!

Numbers!

Now here's where you'll get the most benefit from reading backwards. Not only is reading backwards the single best way to catch transposed or otherwise incorrect numbers, but numbers often make up those parts of a document in which an error can truly be disastrous. I'll admit to you that this is by far the best argument for putting yourself through the tedium of reading backwards.

For this technique to work with numbers, you must truly force yourself to look at each individual digit. Helen O'Guinn uncovers one digit at a time with her finger, moving backwards across a line. To further increase your odds of catching number errors, combine reading backwards with comparison proofreading (comparing your document to another that you know contains accurate information). Here are the types of errors you will often catch if you're carefully reading backwards:

- ◆ Transposed numbers in dates (February *21* versus *12*).
- ◆ Transposed numbers in figures.
- ◆ Errors in columns of figures.
- ◆ Misplaced decimal points.
- ◆ Missing digits, such as *3 minutes* for *30 minutes*.
- ◆ Missing groups of digits, as *1,000* for *1,000,000*.

♦ Mistyped digits, such as area code *219* for *319*.

♦ Numerals that should be spelled out, and vice versa.

If you're rusty on using numerals versus words for numbers, here are the basic rules.

♦ Use words for the numbers one through ten unless they are used to number sequences.

♦ Use numerals for most numbers above ten, unless they appear at the beginning of a sentence. However, if it is a number that requires more than one word—one hundred and fifty, for example—rewrite the sentence so that the number is not the first word.

♦ Use numerals for combinations of half and whole numbers: 2 ½.

♦ Use words for *one million*, *one billion*, etc. when expressed as round figure, (but not *one million two hundred thousand*).

♦ Use numerals or words consistently with numbers appearing in the same sentence. Pick the method easiest to understand.

Remember the proofreading symbol for "spelling out" to communicate that a numeral should be put in word form:

Order ③ binders from the distribution

center.

To indicate that the word form should be a numeral instead, circle the word(s) and attach a circled note:

Order ⟨thirteen⟩ binders from the bookstore. *(use numeral)*

Special kinds of documents may call for straying from the basic rules; many instructional manuals use numerals almost exclusively, for instance, because readers grasp numerals more quickly and tend to remember them. Organization or industry-specific style guides should help you further in proofreading for the correct use of numbers.

Other special problems

Finally, reading backwards can help you catch inconsistencies in style. But you have to be looking for particular kinds of problems. Many organizations handle abbreviations differently; for instance, *Washington, D.C.,* and *Washington, DC,* have both become acceptable ways to spell our nation's capital. Reading backwards is the only sure-fire way to catch these types of inconsistencies involving punctuation and spacing.

Step 5: Scan the document at arm's length

The impact of the visual impression a document makes is grossly underestimated by most writers. Here I'm not talking about obvious ink smears or mistakes crossed or sloppily "whited out" (though those issues are certainly important); other issues of visual impact can make no less important a first and lasting impression. Perhaps more important, they can make reading the document easier.

Remember here that your reader will especially notice text near larger-than-normal areas of white space: bulleted lists, columns of numbers, quotes or addresses "set in" and centered on the page, and headlines and subheads. These elements deserve one last glance, at arm's length, to detect omissions, errors, alignment problems, and areas where your writer's impact could be stronger. The other aspect of the document deserving special attention is any usual treatment of typestyle.

At this final step in the proofreading process, your goal is to pull back from looking at individual words or lines. You should be scanning the various "chunks" of text, looking for these types of problems:

◆ Missing segments of a document (for instance, a return address or date in a business letter).

◆ References to attachments or enclosures not included.

◆ Page or chapter references inconsistent with a table of contents or other segments of the document.

◆ Consistent adherence to any established format (for instance, the full block letter style).

◆ Inconsistent margins.

◆ Inconsistent vertical (up and down) spacing.

◆ Typos in headlines: These command a lot of authority and proofreaders often miss them!

◆ Consistent and appropriate use of font types and sizes.

◆ Appropriate and minimal (for emphasis only) use of italics, boldface, underlining, etc.

◆ Misnumbered sequences.

◆ Consistent alignment of columns, bulleted lists, and indented elements.

◆ Columns of figures with decimals misaligned.

◆ Dollar figures without dollar signs.

◆ Missing titles, labels, or legends in charts or graphs.

This is not an exhaustive list, but instead, a good place to start. You may have other issues you'd like to add (especially issues that repeatedly come up for your author or organization).

Then once you've tackled the now obvious visual impression problems, you might also look further to suggest ways to improve the document's effectiveness and readability (if your author is open to such suggestions, of course). Look for:

- ♦ Long paragraphs that could be split into shorter ones (readers appreciate short paragraphs!).

- ♦ Critical instructions or information buried in the middle of a long paragraph; it won't be seen. (Move it or make it its own paragraph, perhaps.)

- ♦ Opportunities for bulleted lists.

- ♦ Lists that could use bullets or numbering. (Numbering is appropriate when the steps have a definite order.)

- ♦ Addresses, phone numbers, or other information that could be "set in" for the reader's easy reference.

- ♦ Areas where headings could help the reader maneuver through a long document or long segment of information.

Even proofreaders can express a little creativity here. Remember, the proofreader is often in the best position to see these problems or enhancements.

Now that you've tackled all five steps in the proofreading process, take a break. You deserve it! I only hope your author will truly appreciate all the hard work you've given his or her document. Of course, that may not be the case. But that's another story, one I'll address in Chapter 9.

7

A proofreader's guide to punctuation

Certain aspects of punctuation are problematic for many, if not most, working professionals. Often an individual is singled out as a proofreader in an organization simply because he or she is more confident than most in how to use punctuation to communicate effectively.

On the other hand, if punctuation is a challenge for you, you'll probably enjoy only limited success as a proofreader until you gain some knowledge and practice with the rules of punctuation. A good resource for this is a companion book in this series, *Punctuation Plain and Simple* by Edgar C. and Jean A. Alward.

Here I'll mention only the particularly challenging marks a proofreader should watch out for; these are the marks your friends and colleagues are most likely to have difficulty with. As mentioned earlier, many punctuation errors are easier to detect when reading aloud. Others, frankly, are not and require careful reading both forward and backwards.

In examples throughout this section, I've used proofreaders' marks to insert or replace needed punctuation.

Commas

Commas prove to be particularly challenging for most writers, probably because we've always remembered and took to heart the method our first grammar teachers taught us: Commas go where we breathe. While breathing may provide a hint to where a comma might be needed, every breath does not require a comma!

When you're proofreading, reading aloud can help you find many comma errors—provided you're skilled at listening beyond your own breath. In a nutshell, the comma has two primary functions, according to the *Gregg Reference Manual*:

> ...it **sets off** nonessential expressions that interrupt the flow of thought..., and it **separates** elements within a sentence to clarify their relationship to one another.

When proofreading for comma errors, you'll find that your writer either overuses or under-uses them—generally consistently. Those who overuse commas almost always practice the breathing method of using commas; those who under-use commas typically have become "comma shy" after years of frustration with comma rules. Here, first, are the key guidelines for using commas to separate sentence elements.

1. Use commas to separate items in a series (of three or more items), including just before the conjunction.

   We were impressed with her frankness, her compassion, and her willingness to help.

2. Use commas to separate—and conclude—items in an address or a three-part date.

   The site we visited on September 7, 1993, was at Rural Route 7, Wichita, Kansas, in God's country.

3. Use a comma before a coordinate conjunction separating two independent clauses.

   Tom read the proposal, but Janet responded.

4. Use a comma after an introductory dependent clause in a complex sentence to separate it from the main (independent) clause. Do not use a comma when the independent clause comes first.

   Because the project was successful, the team plans to work together again.

   Or:
   The team plans to work together again because the project was successful.

5. Use a comma to separate coordinate (could be joined by "and") adjectives.

   Sue has a bold‸new plan for an old book design.

6. Use a comma after a transitional word or phrase at the beginning of a sentence.

   Of course‸we couldn't start without you.

7. Use a comma after long introductory prepositional phrases.

   At that particular moment‸nothing made sense.

8. Use a comma after an introductory participial or infinitive phrase.

   Remembering her supervisor's advice‸she proofread carefully.

   To be sure‸I checked the figures myself.

9. Use commas with direct quotations—language quoted word-for-word.

   Yesterday you said‸"Leave all the files here."

   "Joe‸" you said yesterday‸"Leave the files here."

10. Use commas to prevent misreading but not just to show the need for a pause.

   For a while͜ longer collars were back in style.

   Most of my friends who read͜ read only for fun.

11. Use commas to show the omission of key words.

   The person who finishes first will receive $500; the person who finishes second͜ $300; the person who finishes third͜ $100.

Here are the guidelines for using commas to set off nonessential expressions.

12. Use commas to set off a noun of direct address.

   The bottom line͜ Joe͜ is that we're under budget.

13. Use commas to set off parenthetical words or phrases, which typically interrupt the flow of the sentence for emphasis.

   Our accountant recommends͜ however͜ that we change our bookkeeping system.

14. Use commas to set off nonrestrictive (unnecessary) dependent phrases and clauses.

   Our CEO͜ who was waiting for the bus͜ was growing impatient.

Or:

The man who was waiting for the bus was growing impatient.

15. Use commas to set off nonrestrictive appositives (expressions that redefine or explain nouns or pronouns).

    Our firm's most valuable account, Jones & Co., has been with us for years.

    My son Tim is in law school. (This appositive is restrictive, or necessary, if I have two sons, so don't use commas.)

16. Use commas to set off titles and degrees that immediately follow a person's name.

    Cheryl Toms, Ph.D., disagreed with the analysis.

Periods

The common proofreading challenges related to the use of periods stem from two basic problems:

- ♦ Misstrikes: Instead of a period, the writer or editor hit an adjacent key, typically a comma or slash.

- ♦ Confusion between abbreviations and acronyms.

Degrees and titles, when abbreviated, take periods. If an abbreviation comes at the end of a sentence, use only one period to conclude both.

We just hired Sharon Reed, M.B.A.

Only widely recognized abbreviations should be used in most forms of business communication. Memoranda and internal e-mail tend to allow for a less formal style, but all other forms of business and academic communication should limit its use of abbreviations that are not widely used. The proofreading mark used to indicate that an abbreviation should be spelled out is used in the example below.

The dept. assistant checks the mail daily.

Acronyms differ from abbreviations in that they're pronounced as words. Acronyms are typically all caps and do not take periods. When using acronyms whose meaning may be unclear to readers, spell out the acronym when it's first used, and then follow with the acronym in parentheses. In subsequent references the acronym will be sufficient.

The world is concerned about acquired

immune deficiency syndrome (AIDS).

Some organization names are *abbreviated* to look like acronyms. These, while not pronounced as words, also do not take periods.

The IRS agent works out at the YMCA.

When in doubt about whether you're dealing with an abbreviation, which takes periods, or acronym, which doesn't, look it up in a reputable style guide, either a generic guide or one published by your field, industry, or company.

A third problem with periods is generally tackled at the editing stage: Compound and complex sentences longer than 14 words or so, even if correctly punctuated, may be easier to read when separated into simple (one-clause) sentences. But be careful here because chopping every compound and complex sentence into a simple sentence can create an uneven, hard-to-read flow. Both concise writing and sentence variety contribute to effective communication.

Double space after all terminal (or ending) punctuation, including after periods, and also after colons, which we'll discuss next. There's one exception to this rule. If you're involved in getting material published, leave the extra spaces out. Publishers don't use the extra spaces, so they'll have to take them out if you don't.

Semicolons and colons

Semicolons and colons are very commonly misused due to two basic problems:

♦ Misstrikes are common, especially since these marks share the same keyboard key.

♦ Many people confuse the functions of these two marks.

Here, briefly, are the guidelines for using semicolons and colons.

1. Use a semicolon between two independent clauses not joined with a coordinate conjunction. (If one clause already contains commas, use a semicolon—not a comma—even with a coordinate conjunction.)

Tom read the report; Janet responded

Tom, the CEO, read the report; but Janet responded.

2. Use a semicolon to separate items in a series if the items themselves contain commas.

The team included Terry Sams, project manager; Mark Elliott, engineer; and Kathy Parks, surveyor.

3. Use a semicolon between two independent clauses when the second clause explains or illustrates the first.

The job you described sounds attractive; the salary is excellent.

4. Use a colon to introduce items in a series; colons should not follow a preposition or a verb in a regular sentence.

We will open branch offices in these states: Illinois, Michigan, and Ohio.

A colon is always appropriate to introduce a vertical list.

We will open:

- a branch office
- a sales office
- a distribution center

5. Use a colon when the first clause introduces the clause or clauses that follow.

    Here are the tools you will need: a

    hammer, a screwdriver, and pliers.

6. Use a colon after the salutation of a business letter.

    Ladies and Gentlemen:

    Dear Mr. Ames:

    Dear Terry Ames:

Quotation marks

All paired punctuation marks warrant a proofreader's close attention because the partner mark is often missing. Of all the paired marks (which include quotes, parentheses, and sometimes dashes), quotation marks seem to cause the most confusion. Here, briefly are guidelines for using both double and single quotes.

1. Enclose in quotation marks language quoted word-for-word. The first word of a direct quote is always capitalized.

    Yesterday you said, "Leave all the files here."

    Remarks paraphrased should not be enclosed in quotation marks.

    Yesterday you said I should leave all the

    files here.

2. Use quotation marks around words referring to words (for example, the box was marked "fragile"). These can also be underlined or put in italics instead. The quote typically begins with a capital (though style guides disagree on whether the capital letter is necessary).

He stamped the invoice "Paid."

Writers are often confused about where punctuation at the end of a quote should go in relation to the quotation mark. Here goes: Periods and commas always go *inside* end quotation marks; semicolons and colons always go *outside*; question marks or exclamation points go *inside or outside* depending on the material quoted. If the whole sentence is quoted, they go inside; if only a part of the sentence is quoted, the question mark or exclamation point goes on the outside of the quotation mark.

Did the contractor say, "Yes, of course"?

The contractor asked, "What does this mean?"

3. Enclose book chapters or magazine articles in quotation marks. The title of the magazine or book itself should be underlined or put in italics.

I read an article called "Better Project Management in Engineering Today." *ital.*

4. When quoting inside a quote, use single quotation marks.

I told him, "Don't drop that; it's marked 'Fragile.'"

Ellipsis marks

Ellipsis marks (three spaced periods) should be used to show the omission of a word or words, generally from a direct quote. Follow ellipsis marks at the end of a sentence or fragment with a fourth period (or other ending punctuation) to show both the omission of material and the end of the thought.

> **"The commission discussed bridge construction...and roadway projects."**

> **Try to put these punctuation rules into practice....**

Parentheses

Proofreaders should beware of three key problems writers typically have with parentheses:

♦ Writers forget the closing parenthesis.

♦ Writers use them in place of commas or dashes to enclose *all* nonessential sentence elements.

♦ Writers have difficulty with punctuation near the closing parenthesis.

Overused parentheses. Parentheses around words indicate that the words are unimportant or unnecessary. Therefore, they should not be used often. Many writers have the misperception that any expression that is not essential to the basic meaning of a sentence must be enclosed in parentheses. Commas are generally more appropriate for those situations. Parentheses communicate to a reader, "Go right ahead and skip this; in fact, I'm not even sure I needed to include it."

Tom and I (determined to succeed) worked overtime every day last week.

We (Tom and I) discussed that at our last meeting.

Punctuation with ending parenthesis. When the parentheses enclose only part of the sentence, any punctuation that follows the parentheses goes outside the closing mark. Also, the first word enclosed in parentheses is not capitalized, even if what you're enclosing could stand alone as a full sentence. Finally, sentences enclosed in other sentences lose their ending punctuation, unless it's a question mark or exclamation point.

We discussed the timelines at our last meeting (two weeks ago).

We discussed the timelines (you were part of that discussion) at our last meeting.

When the parentheses enclose an idea to be treated as a separate sentence, the period goes inside the closing mark and the first word in parentheses is capitalized. The previous example could also have been handled this way:

We discussed the timelines at our last meeting. (You were part of that discussion.)

Omitted closing parenthesis. Good proofreaders get into the habit of expecting the closing marks to be missing from any paired set. And writers tend to leave out closing parentheses more often than quotes or dashes. Reading aloud can help catch these because when we read words in parentheses aloud, we naturally inflect our voice differently. Here's another trick: Put a left index finger on any opening parenthesis you come to, and don't lift it until you find its partner.

A closing parenthesis can appear alone, however, when it's used following a number as in a sequence of steps:

1) **Type in your account number.**

2) **Press ENTER.**

The closing parenthesis, when used this way, replaces the period.

Brackets. For parentheses within parentheses, use brackets ([ ]). However, do this sparingly as it can make your writing cluttered and difficult to follow.

(We discussed the timelines at our last meeting. We[Tom and I]met two weeks ago.)

Brackets are also used within quotes to enclose brief explanatory notes and *sic* (italicized), which indicates that a misspelling, a grammar error, or other unclear language existed in the original material and has not been corrected.

Tom said, "I ain't a-goin' [*sic*] into that cave!"

Dashes (em dashes)

Dashes should be used—sparingly—for emphasis or interruption. A dash (also called an em dash because it's the width of an *m*) is two hyphens typed without spaces between, before, or after them. Many word processing programs now convert the two hyphens into an actual dash.

> John conducted the meeting Terry couldn't
>
> be there on Tuesday morning.

Another way to indicate the need for a dash is to use the em dash symbol.

> John conducted the meeting Terry couldn't
>
> be there on Tuesday morning.

Dashes don't always come in pairs. If the punctuation needed after the dashed material is a comma, use the closing dash instead. If the punctuation needed is a colon, semicolon, or a closing parenthesis, use that punctuation instead of the closing dash.

> I delivered the report by noon—just as I
>
> promised but John wasn't in that day.

> I delivered the report by noon—just as I
>
> promised but John wasn't in that day.

Hyphens

Check for hyphens in some compound words, two or more words used together to form an *adjective phrase* immediately before a noun or pronoun, and in word breaks at the end of a line of text—but use word breaks sparingly; they can be jarring to the reader.

> *Avoid:* **We're working on a three͞ mile͞ long**
> ‸   ‸
> **roadway.**

> *Use:*   **The roadway is three miles long.**

Hyphens between numbers (en dashes)

Hyphens separating numbers can be very difficult to see. So a second type of dash, called an en dash (because it's the width of an *n*) is often used in computer-generated text to replace the hyphen meaning *to* between two numbers:

> **June 6–13**   **pages 350–355**

The en dash is preferable to a hyphen between two numbers because it's slightly longer and easier to see. Many word processing programs now include the en dash as a special character writers can insert. Whether you're using the en dash or a hyphen, don't space before or after them.

Because an en dash is rather unknown outside the publishing industry, when calling for one as a proofreader, be sure to include a circled note.

> **June 6͞ 13** *(insert en dash)*   **pages 350͞ 355** *(replace with en dash)*
> ‸

Apostrophes

Apostrophes tend to be the mark of punctuation writers most often leave out. Check for apostrophes in contractions and possessive nouns—but not possessive pronouns like *its*. Apostrophes are not used to form plurals (except the plurals of single letters, for example: dot your *i*'s and cross your *t*'s).

Make singular nouns possessive by adding -*'s*. Use the same rule for plural nouns not ending in -*s*. For plural nouns ending in -*s*, add only the apostrophe after the -*s*.

a contractors decision

several contractors decisions

a mans suit   **two mens suits**

Some writers get confused when creating plural possessive nouns from singular nouns ending in *s*. The rules, however, are the same: The owner is first made plural, then possessive.

Use: **the Joneses' house**

Not: **the Jones' house**

Many other writers are confused by singular possessives ending in *s*. Style guides can help you choose the best option when faced with odd singular possessives such as the following:

Mr. Jones's coat

The regular approach is best when the possessive would result in pronouncing an extra syllable.

But:

Euripides's journey

Leave the last *s* off when the word it would create would be awkward to pronounce.

While this has been an abbreviated tour through the rules of punctuation, it should well serve the proofreader already feeling pretty comfortable with punctuation rules. But if punctuation is challenging for you, it's only a start and you'll want to continue to develop your skills. The good news is that as with so many things in life, one of the best ways to enhance a set of skills is to put yourself in a position to practice using them. You'll learn what you need to know along the way.

8

Tips for screen proofing (when you must)

E-mail; computer-generated faxes; messages via bulletin boards, online forums, the Internet...these days most of us are communicating electronically at least as often as we're passing paper. Our ever-evolving means of transferring technological information raise new issues: What constitutes effective communication? What standards of accuracy should we maintain? These newer forms of communication have transferred and even stretched the rules of informality we used to apply only to memos and the notes we passed around the office to almost any office around the world. Now everyone can be part of our virtual office.

What should the new standard of effective communication and accuracy be? Should it truly be less formal, almost as if we're speaking to one another? If this is the case, we need not worry so much about the absolute accuracy of every word, letter, and punctuation mark. Or should we treat these communications as we would a formal business letter with all the *i*'s dotted and *t*'s crossed, to use a now-very-old saying? Arguments can be made in both directions.

For or against "casual" communication?

If you're a frequent e-mail user, you've come to enjoy its many virtues: its convenience; its speed in getting a message out, especially to many people at once; its potential for quick response; and its versatility (many systems allow you to attach entire files to messages, for instance). You probably use it, in fact, because more than any other type of written communication, e-mail most closely resembles voice-to-voice communication. (Some people even try to instill an emotional flavor in their messages with "smileys"—for example, :-) is used to represent a smile.) E-mail, one might argue, allows for immediate feedback from a recipient in almost the same way a gasp on the other end of a phone line tells us we've shocked that person by something we've said. And if this immediate feedback is possible, must our message be absolutely perfect the first time out? After all, if someone's confused about an e-mail message, won't he or she simply respond with a question?

Besides, the argument might go, people expect e-mail to be a more casual form of communication. It's intended to more spontaneous, more urgent, more action-provoking than either a letter or a memorandum. One should use it to get a message out faster without having to worry about all those conventions of formal language. Given its nature, people forgive the occasional typos. That's the nature of the electronic game.

I'll argue, however, that this get-it-out-now nature is one of the most important reasons to proofread e-mail messages. If you've ever had that panicked feeling immediately after sending off a message you hadn't quite thought through, you know what I'm talking about. Afterthoughts, second thoughts (oh, I hope so-and-so doesn't take that the wrong way), details you meant to double-check—there's no better potential for virtual embarrassment.

Couple this with the fact that we're often sending these messages to wide distribution lists, and that even those not intended to see the message can generally do so. There's no such thing as a small embarrassment online.

I'll agree that people do expect less formality and more spontaneity in e-mail communication. Most people do forgive the occasional, innocuous typo. But the question is: Are you sure they got the message precisely as you intended it? Especially when you composed it so spontaneously? And if they misunderstood something, can you be sure either you or they would even know it?

I disagree that people *always* respond immediately when they have a question—or that they always realize they've misunderstood something in the first place. The truth is, written communication—in any form—will never be as foolproof as communication that's face-to-face or even voice-to-voice. Most communication studies tell us that the actual words account for only 7 to 12 percent of the message we're hoping to convey. Human beings respond much more readily to a message conveyed by body language (for instance, crossed arms) or the tone of someone's voice. Those types of communication *assure* both sender and receiver that we got the message across.

When we're communicating online we don't have the benefit of a confused look, or a spontaneous "What?" on the other end of a phone line. In this sense, in spite of smileys, electronic communication is more like writing a memo or letter than making a phone call.

Keeping an audience's interest online

So many of us are dealing with such vast networks of people sending so many message every day that we're developing an aversion to reading e-mail messages. Think of how you read your e-mail. Do you read it carefully, word-for-word? Or do you scan it? Do you even scan most of it? Most people I talk to about the writing in their organizations admit they have to scan e-mail messages or they'd do nothing but read e-mail.

Most e-mail messages are too long, often irrelevant, and slow to get to the point, with subject lines too generic to be helpful. Take this example, which a writing workshop participant from a large, well-known company, shared with me:

Date:	Tuesday, 19 November 19XX 6:43pm CT
To:	XXXX.XXX.TEAM, XXXX.XXX.TEST, XXXX.XXX.STAFF, XXXX.XX.STAFF, *
Cc:	John.XXX
From:	XXXX.XXX
Subject:	Removal of files from the 4th floor

We will begin removing files from the 4th floor tomorrow. We will start with the corporate E/I files continue around with Special Markets into GAA enrollments. We will not be taking enrollment cards. Only cases with enrollments / investment option forms. After all of the enrollment and investment option forms have been removed, we will take the benefit files. We already have XXX's benefits down here currently doing a first half of the year purge. We will pick up corporate benefits and special markets 2nd half of the year and bring them down here. We will purge special markets benefits for the first half of the year and send to the XXXXX building.

Upon completion of those files, everyone hopefully will have their fact sheets made for the premium files so we can bring the premium files down together. We are fully aware there is filing piling up on the teams. In order to take this filing down here as we take these files we ask a few things of the teams...

When did you stop reading? Now, I realize comprehending another company's alphabet soup of acronyms and jargon is especially challenging; however, the person who shared this message with me had just about as much trouble with it, and it directly affected her. (By the way, I've included only about half of the original message.)

Most people scan e-mail messages—if they're not too frustrated by them. And people tend to learn quickly whose messages to skip and whose to take seriously. E-mail messages, like memos and letters, help determine your reputation as an effective or ineffective communicator. They simply determine it faster and among more people.

The bottom line then is this: We can't afford not to proofread (and edit, for that matter) our online communications. We have far too much at stake. While proofreading on screen is in many ways more challenging, it is well worth the effort to learn to do it effectively.

Difficulties of proofreading on screen

As I mentioned in Chapter 2, even expert proofreaders say they can't proofread as effectively on screen as on paper. Our eyes don't seem to single out errors as well on screen as on paper, perhaps because the computer strains the eyes more or because we tend to attach more authority to words coming to us from a screen. I feel at a disadvantage proofreading on screen simply because I can't hold the document in my hands, move it closer to my eyes, put a finger on the text when I need to. In fact, I have trouble simply keeping my eyes on one line of text at time. I suspect I'm not alone.

Yet printing every e-mail message you write might not be practical (although I'd still recommend it for a message that must be flawless). If you're composing on screen, and the document will ultimately appear in printed form, I'd strongly recommend proofreading on paper. If you don't, your reader has a definite advantage over you at seeing the errors. In fact, the only situation in which I'd even consider proofreading on screen is one in which what I'm creating will never appear in paper form. So while printing a copy of a file might be inconvenient, every proofreader I've ever talked to says it's worth the effort.

When you're faced with proofreading on screen, however, you can take certain steps to increase the likelihood you'll catch everything. The rest of this chapter is devoted to tips that will help you increase your effectiveness proofreading on screen. Let's begin with the characteristics of effective on-screen text, and then discuss tools and tips for proofreading on screen.

Characteristics of effective on-screen text

Your on-screen text may take the form of e-mail; a computer-generated fax; messages on a bulletin board, online forum, or the Internet; or other technologies most of us aren't even aware of yet. These forms of electronic communication typically vary in their abilities to provide easy-to-read text. For instance, some e-mail software doesn't distinguish between upper- and lowercase letters; bulletin boards and online forums don't always allow you flexibility with spacing. To the extent you can control any of the following text characteristics, doing so will improve both your and your readers' ability to quickly comprehend your message. The most effective on-screen text:

♦ Includes both upper- and lower-case letters.

Typing text in all capitals may take slightly less time (and fudging on the capitalization rules is convenient), but normal text is easier to read and less alienating. Text in all caps tends to scream at your readers, and no one likes to be screamed at.

♦ Includes plenty of white space.

Ample white space means writing short, concise sentences and paragraphs. Also, double space between paragraphs (even if they're single-line paragraphs). Doing so makes reading easier. And finally, consider setting important information in from the margins in a bulleted list or centered as you might an important address in a letter.

♦ Gets right to the point right up front.

This tenet of all good writing is especially important when your intended readers have far too many messages to page through and the convenience of a single key to not do so.

♦ Contains a concise, but specific subject line.

Because subject lines typically serve as indexes from which readers select messages relevant to them, a well-written subject line can go a long way in making you friends (or enemies) online.

♦ Is directed at a small, relevant distribution.

Don't frustrate readers who don't need to see your message, even if this means taking the time to list individual names. By doing this you will avoid developing a reputation for frivolously taking up your co-workers' time.

♦ Contains clear, strong, and concise language.

These are the principles of good editing; don't overlook their importance to getting a reader to read your message. (See Chapter 4.)

♦ Contains no errors, ideally; no important errors, definitely.

Important errors, as we discussed in Chapter 6, are those errors that carry consequences: dangerous or costly misunderstandings, embarrassment, or a loss of credibility. The answer here, of course, is good proofreading.

Use the computer to your advantage

One clear advantage to on-screen proofreading is the vast array of tools a computer has to offer:

♦ Cut and paste features of your software.

Learn the shortcuts (software always has shortcuts) so editing and proofreading are as effortless as possible. Global replace features, which allow you to search for and replace a repeated element with minimal key strokes, can be especially time-saving.

♦ Spell-checkers.

Even most e-mail systems now have a spell-checking feature. Yes, it takes extra time, but use it—you're even less likely to pick up the tough-to-catch spelling errors and duplicate words on screen than on paper. Don't rely on your spell-checker as an all-in-one proofreading tool, however. Even the best spell-checkers have limitations. Know the limitations of yours, and follow up spell-checking with solid proofreading.

♦ Grammar-checkers.

If you find the grammar-checking feature of your software helpful, use it. My preference is to skip the grammar-checker, but perhaps I just haven't found one yet that yields more editing value for less time spent.

♦ Text-marking features.

If you're editing or proofreading for someone else or making changes a team or individual will approve first, check out the text-marking feature available on most word processing software. Text-marking allows you to make changes, which appear as cross-outs and additions to the document. Generally this feature can be turned on or off with a keystroke or two.

Using text-marking is a little tricky at first; every misstroke is recorded as an addition or deletion. But when several individuals are involved in pulling a document together, it can be a useful team tool.

Tips for on-screen proofreading

The basic proofreading steps work as well for screen as for paper proofing. As we discussed in Chapter 6, when time is short, the single most important step is undoubtedly Step 2, reading the text slowly aloud. Again, doing so may seem awkward to you at first. Without a doubt, though, it is the single quickest way to find most errors in a document.

Here are a few more tips for on-screen proofreading:

♦ Use your cursor to help focus your attention.

♦ Page down one line at a time.

♦ Enlarge the text while proofreading it to make it easier to read.

Problematic on-screen errors

Certain types of errors tend to be more of a problem with on-screen text computing. If you can take a second look for trouble spots, you might look first for these:

♦ Spacing problems.

Less sophisticated word processing software, such as that in e-mail systems, sometimes create inconsistent spacing across lines of text. Check especially for these gaps or absences of space. If your software allows for a "justification" setting, be sure to select left justification, which creates an even left margin but a natural (ragged) right one, never full justification. Full justification stretches text across a line so both margins appear even, but it creates inconsistent spacing within the lines, which is more difficult to read.

♦ Word wrap problems.

Word wrap refers to the way a word processing software treats text at the ends of lines. Less sophisticated systems end the lines after a certain number of digits, regardless of whether you're in the middle of a word. If you're faced with this problem, take the time to create more reasonable line breaks with hyphens and extra space. Yes, it's a hassle, but reading will be easier. When it really becomes a hassle, talk to your technology people (if you have them).

Be aware that even e-mail systems with word wrap often don't print text as neatly as it appears on the screen. While that's certainly not ideal, it really doesn't hinder your proofreading that dramatically, and the many advantages to proofreading on paper far outweigh this disadvantage. By all means, don't use this shortcoming as an excuse not to proofread on paper when you have the opportunity.

♦ Ghosts of old phrasing you rejected but failed to delete.

♦ Domino-effect problems, again the result of changing your mind; change a singular subject to plural and you'll need to change the verb too.

♦ Missing segments of sentences, often the result of copying text with repeated words from one document to another.

♦ Poor typing habits or other writer-specific tendencies for errors. Since proofreading on screen is less foolproof than proofreading on paper, you'd best assume the writer, too, missed blatant, even repetitive errors.

♦ New text inserted in the wrong place, creating gibberish.

More how-to tips

Here are a few final tips for proofreading on screen.

♦ With long documents, work in short, uninterrupted time frames. Ten minutes is probably the limit for real effectiveness (half of the limit when proofreading on paper).

- Even a short time lapse between composing a message and editing or proofreading it helps you gain a fresh perspective. Save the document so you won't lose it, but then take a short walk.

- Consider having a buddy proofread for you, especially if the message is important. You can even send him or her a draft version first (if you're able to send messages with a relative assurance of confidentiality) before distributing it widely.

- Double-check your tone. Often messages sent in haste are a little more harsh, preachy, or demanding than you might otherwise have wanted them.

- When comparison proofreading, use a document holder to make the job easier—you'll do a better job, too.

Of all the potential liabilities involved in proofreading on screen, the single most critical one is failing to do it. Proofreading makes a difference, especially when you don't do it; others *will* notice even if you don't.

9

Proofreading for others: *do's and don'ts*

The aptitudes, skills, and knowledge proofreading requires, which we discussed in Chapter 2, aren't all that is necessary to be an effective proofreader. Knowing what to mark and how to mark it is only half the battle when you're editing or proofreading for another person. You also have to contend with—well, that other person.

The interpersonal side of proofreading may, in fact, be the most challenging. Many secretaries and administrative assistants proofread for bosses under less than ideal circumstances. Perhaps the boss never really appreciates the effort or time involved in doing the job right. Perhaps she never really wants you to find errors or regularly wants to debate those you find. Or maybe you're proofreading on the sly—the boss really doesn't know or appreciate how horrible or unfinished the writing is before you do your magic. He thinks you're just sticking the thing in an envelope, and his wonderful communications are transforming the masses all on their own.

Or here's another scenario. The word is out that you're the most competent grammarian in the department. Now more and more people are coming to expect you to provide regular editing or proofreading services. Their documents are always urgent priorities. And while assuming this role has been very flattering, it's not part of your job description.

Proofreading is probably one of the least (truly) appreciated roles we can assume in an organization. Everyone wants it done right, needed it done yesterday, and would love someone else to do it so he or she can get on with changing the world.

While I probably can't do much to change the dysfunctional relationships in your work environment, I can offer a few suggestions to make the role you assume as proofreader an easier one—and perhaps even help you gain a little more respect around the office. Here are what I consider the Five Fundamental Principles of Proofreading for Others.

Principle 1: First, do no harm

This may seem obvious, but I've blown even this first principle by marking in ink on a document someone considered a "final version." Even though this is less of a problem now that computers make printing duplicate copies easier, be careful. A document with an original signature or printed on the last piece of letterhead stationery may create a real problem for the author if you mark on it. Another problem I sometimes run into is a document with graphics or other elements manually pasted in. Changes made on these document often mean recutting and pasting!

My solution is simple. I make a point never to mark on an original document. I mark on a copy.

If you've been handed a file on disk, be especially careful. Few authors trust an editor or proofreader to make changes sight unseen. If you share ownership of a document with someone else or a team, make sure everyone's expectations about how changes will be made and any disagreements resolved are clear. One tool your team might consider using is the text-marking feature of many software programs, which allows you to make changes that appear on the document as additions and deletions while retaining the original text. Once team members (or partners) agree on the changes, simply turning off the text-marking feature officially registers final changes.

I've also learned to be very clear with an author (or my team members) about how much marking they can expect to see on a document I'm proofreading or (especially) editing. This issue leads me to Principle 2.

Principle 2: Make sure your input is wanted

Different people have different concepts of what "reviewing" or "critiquing" or "giving feedback on" a document is all about. Whenever you're in the position of editing or proofreading for someone (especially if it's the first time), make sure you know what level of feedback the writer's expecting. Many competent proofreaders take for granted that an author asking for feedback really wants a thorough job of it. But I know plenty of folks who, regardless of how horrible their writing, seek out "proofreaders" but want nothing more than a nod of reassurance.

Clarify this with an author by talking *specifically* about the kinds of problems you'd typically look for and whether or not those match his or her expectations. You might even take this opportunity to show the author your proof-readers' marks (see Chapter 5). Doing so at this point accomplishes several goals:

♦ It establishes a common language for communicating on paper with the author.

♦ It dramatically helps clarify expectations between editor and author by making the abstract request ("critique this document") more concrete.

♦ It can help clarify who "owns" the document and therefore has the final say with regard to changes.

♦ It will raise issues related to harming the document (if those have not yet surfaced) and whether or not you should make "permanent" markings.

♦ It begins the process of establishing a partnership between author and editor. (I'll discuss this more in Principle 5.)

And what about those authors who ask for feedback but either don't really want it (or not much of it, anyway) or don't really have time to incorporate your suggestions?

I respond to this all-too-common scenario a couple of ways, depending on who truly owns the document. In other words, if I have a vested interest in the content of the document, for instance, if errors in the document could directly affect me (my company, my department, etc.) in what I consider a significant way, I insist we take the time to get it right. In a way, I partially own this document even if I didn't compose it.

On the other hand, if the document truly belongs to the author, he or she makes the call. Then I try to help as much as I can. If we only have time for a cursory look, I read the document (out loud) for gross inaccuracies and problems of clarity. I also try to spot check those "most critical" errors we discussed in Chapter 6. For instance, I always try to verify the spellings of clients' names, products, or organizations. And I take a second look at any numbers, especially those next to dollar signs.

Finally, what about those situations in which the author is more than open to your suggestions; in fact, he or she would just have you rewrite the document if you so desire? Well, if doing so benefits you in some way (for instance, you can expect the favor returned at some point in the future or you could gain brownie points with someone important...), do it. More often, however, these requests come from co-workers who wouldn't mind dumping their work (perhaps especially if it involves writing!) into your lap. Again, be careful.

With these co-workers, I again limit my suggestions to those most critical issues. Often, I even do this on the fly, as they're still standing there, next to my desk. If I agree to really review the document, I first insist that we take the time afterward to discuss my comments. I give *myself* a time limit I won't go beyond. And I make more suggestions than actual changes. For instance, I may circle a passage and label it "confusing" but not take the time to fix it. Or I'll explain the problem verbally and then tactfully pass the responsibility for fixing it back to the author. Sometimes this strategy involves working with the author to fix the first instance of a problem. Then I encourage the author to take it from there.

Principle 3: Show sensitivity—always

Editors should always remember how we humans tend to respond to criticism: We abhor it. Yes, most of us can take it, and most of us realize it can help us grow professionally and personally, but we still hate it. Couple this trait of human nature with the fact that people tend to mistakenly equate language problems (especially those involving grammar and punctuation) with a lack of intelligence, and you, as an editor, are in a powerful but dangerous position. Especially in a business environment, where maintaining working relationships is so important, editors must be aware of their potential effect on an author's self-esteem. Here are a few ideas for getting the editing done without destroying the author in the process:

♦ Never, *never* use a red pen to edit.

Do you remember the last teacher who bled all over a document into which you'd so painstakingly poured your time and energy? Perhaps you were a kid then. Adults, even more than kids, tie their self-esteem to what they can do. And to almost all of us, red ink means you can't do this; you screwed up.

Trust me, pick a different color of ink. You'll keep more friends around the office.

♦ Mention (or comment in the margin about) strengths in the writing.

Find something good (and believable) to comment on. Almost any author then can find the less positive feedback easier to take. This suggestion is especially important when you're working with an author for the first time, you know the author is rather thin-skinned, or your markings are extensive.

Treat the author-editor relationship as a partnership. This concept is so important, I've called it Principle 5. More on this there.

♦ Help the author focus and fix what matters most.

A document that need not be absolutely perfect may not be worth overwhelming an author with every suggestion you can pull out of your back pocket.

Show him or her the most critical errors. For instance, don't mention a missing hyphen (which most people overlook anyway) when the entire document needs an overhaul.

If you have an on-going opportunity to work together, make an informal agreement to help the author polish up the writing a little more with each project. If you won't have such an on-going relationship, mention that the document could be polished further, but reassure him or her that you've caught the really critical stuff.

♦ Admit your own limitations.

No one has all the answers. No one does a flawless job every single time.

When you don't know something, admit it, and then model looking it up. Exposing the author to resources you use when you're not sure about something can only help save you both time in the future.

If you make a mistake, own up to it. I do, and I don't believe I've ever lost credibility because of it.

Principle 4: Do a competent job

Authors trust their editors and proofreaders. Let them down (beyond the occasional mistake, which everyone's entitled to), and they lose confidence not only in you, but perhaps even in their own abilities. After all, if *you're* the "expert," and *you* screw up royally...

Those taking on the role of editor or proofreader must assume responsibility for being and staying informed on the rules of language. If your grammar skills are generally strong, but you've never really had a handle on using active versus passive voice, you owe it to those you edit for to upgrade your skills.

Some of the best ways I can suggest for staying informed (and valuable as an editor and proofreader) are:

♦ Continually look up language problems you're not completely sure about.

♦ Occasionally look up language problems you *are* sure about. Take seriously any disagreements an author raises with your corrections, especially if you get this feedback from more than one person. Could a rule have changed? Could it apply differently in a different context?

♦ Be prepared to back up those points whose accuracy you've verified. If necessary, have a page reference memorized. Those obnoxious individuals we all know who'll always doubt our judgments generally can't argue with solid references.

♦ Acknowledge any language weaknesses, even less than perfect spelling, and work to correct them over time.

Editors and proofreaders can also increase their effectiveness by keeping lists of common types of problems their authors continue to struggle with. These lists should help provide focus, especially when editing or proofreading time is limited. Some types of errors can even be searched for and replaced globally (by using word processing software).

And avoid hedging your bets by agreeing to edit or proofread handwritten copy or copy on a computer screen. Text on paper gives you at least a fighting chance.

Principle 5: Work to create a partnership

The most ineffective working relationships I know involve an autocrat and (generally) the autocrat's underling. If you're in a supervisory position, for instance, one of the worst mistakes you can make with a staff member is undermining his or her authority (on paper and otherwise). Don't overrule the author's phrasing without a valid reason.

The *most* effective working relationships I know involve partnerships between two individuals, regardless of their positions on the organizational chart.

In the relationship between an editor or proofreader and an author, partnership means demonstrating the following characteristics:

♦ Inherent agreement that both individuals share interest in, and responsibility for producing a sound document.

♦ Initial agreement on the ground rules; the level of feedback sought, for instance.

♦ A common understanding of the markings used and the manner of editing (for instance, if the document must be edited or proofread on screen, is text marking warranted?).

♦ Agreement to discuss issues that are unclear or that likely will bring disagreement.

♦ When beneficial, shared access to information (for instance, access to business cards or reports so verifying proper names or important numbers is easy).

♦ Consistent respect for both roles in the process, which involves consistent attention to all Five Fundamental Principles of Proofreading for Others.

One proofreading expert has described the skills of proofreading as "interpersonal" skills; indeed they are. For regardless of your aptitude for proofreading, your relevant technical skills and knowledge (of punctuation, spelling, capitalization, and the like), or the specific approach (or set of steps you choose to use), your true effectiveness as a proofreader really does come down to one thing: Are you able to communicate what you know to be right in a way that others are willing to accept?

Proofreading carries with it the responsibility of helping others achieve their communication goals. In order to do so successfully, you will need to constantly improve your skills and strategies. Putting to use all you have learned here is a great step towards achieving that goal.

Appendix

Answers to Chapter 5 exercises

Practice deleting words, characters, and punctuation

1. We never do any~~any~~anything well till we cease to thin~~g~~k about~~t~~ the manner~~n~~ ~~the~~ ~~manner~~ of doing it.

   —William Hazlitt

2. The easiest~~/~~ person~~/~~ to deceive is one's~~s~~ own self.

   —Edward Bulwer-Lytton

Practice inserting words and characters

1. To be, or no*t* to be, tha*t* *the* is question.

   —William Shakespeare

   The close-up hooks connecting the t to tha prevent misreading the change as a Shakespearean tis.

2. Correct th*i*s ser*i*es of numbers:

   18   19   20   2*1*   22   23   2*4*   25

3. *early to rise)* Early to bed and makes wealthy, and *a man healthy,)*
   wise.

   —Ben Franklin

4. The occasional err*o*r is *a* tool for ~~edcaton~~ *education*.

Practice inserting punctuation

1. He used a hammer*,* nails*,* and glue to repair Ed*'*s window*.*

   The alternative mark for inserting a period is ⊗.

2. Wasn*'*t the memo sent to Sandy*,* president*;* Pete*,* vice president*;* and Larry*,* treasurer*?*

3. Bring two items to class*:* a notebook and a pen*.*

4. Ed will like the state of the art look of his new window⊙

5. Remember these symbols of the 60s, tie= dyed shirts and peace signs, oh, what memories!

   You might also have indicated the dash with /M

6. Hank was in school during these years 1980-1985⊙

Practice replacing words, characters, and punctuation

1. ~~Gud punktuwation~~ Good punctuation skills are important to good proophreading.

   Replacing the entire word <u>good</u> *is easier to read than simply replacing the* <u>u</u> *with* <u>oo</u>, *though you could also have approached it that way.*

2. Commas, not semicolons enclose unnecessarie phrases.

3. Where ~~theirs~~ there's marriage with love, there will be love without ~~marage~~ marriage.

   —Ben Franklin

   You might also have opted to insert <u>ri</u> *into* <u>marage</u>.

Paradise
4. ~~Pair a dice~~ is were I am /⊙

—Voltaire

Practice closing, reducing, and inserting space

1. Too err is humman, to for give divine.

—Alexander Pope

2. Writ ing isn't sohard; no harder than ditch- digging.

—Patrick Dennis

3. The plan his friend gave him grewtoo tall.

4. Ifonly computers could proof read!

Practice transposing words, characters, and punctuation

1. Laugh yourself at first, before anyone eles can.

—Elsa Maxwell

2. Learning is a which will treasure follow its owner everywhere.

—Chinese proverb

Transposing two words for one is acceptable if the transposition remains clear.

3. A ~~money~~ ^{fool} and his ~~fool~~ ^{money} are soon parted.
— ~~61~~st Century saying

4. We can |lessons draw| from the past, but
~~cannot we~~ ^{We cannot} live in it.

—B. Lyndon Johnson

Replacing is easier to read than transposing when the transposed words appear on two separate lines.

Practice deleting, inserting, replacing, transposing, and moving text

1. It is a mistake to look too far ahead Only one link in the chain of destiny can be handled at a time.

—Winston Churchill

2. This time, like all times is a very ~~very~~ good one, if ~~know~~ we know what to do with it.

—Ralph Waldo Emerson

3. Time is dead as long as it is being clicked off by little wheels; only when the clock stops does time come to life.

—William Faulkner

4. Jack of all ~~none~~ trades and master ~~trades.~~ of none.

—Maria Edgeworth

Practice capitalizing, making lower case, and spelling out

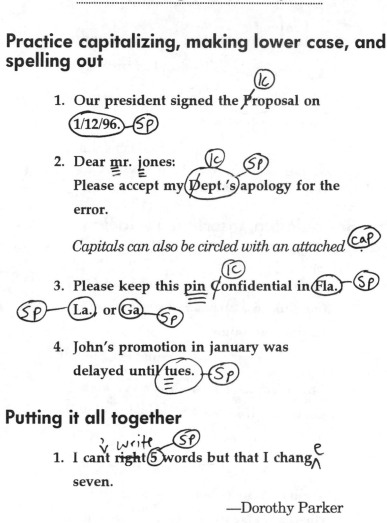

1. Our president signed the Proposal on *(lc)* 1/12/96. *(sp)*

2. Dear mr. jones: *(lc)* *(sp)*
   Please accept my Dept.'s apology for the error.

   Capitals can also be circled with an attached (cap)

3. Please keep this pin confidential in Fla. *(lc)* *(sp)*
   (sp) La. or Ga *(sp)*

4. John's promotion in january was delayed until tues. *(sp)*

Putting it all together

1. I cant right 5 words but that I change seven. *(write)(sp)*

   —Dorothy Parker

2. Did you know the italian word ciao *ital.*
   literally means I am yur slave? *no ital.*

3. Only an mediocre writter always at his best.

   —W. Somerset Maugham

4. Our blunders mostly come from leting
   our ~~wisshs~~ wishes intrepret our ~~dutys~~ duties.

   —Anonymous

5. ~~Their~~ There is nothing final about a mistake,
   except it's being taken as final.

   —Phyllis Bottome

6. if you would not be forgotten, as soon as
   you are dead and rotten, either write
   things worth reading, do or things
   worth the writing.

   —Benjamin Franklin

Index